T0209989

God's divine alignment / God's divine assignment

REV. MICHAEL DAY

WESTBOW
PRESS®
A DIVISION OF THOMAS NELSON
& ZONDERVAN

WestBow Press books may be ordered through booksellers or by contacting:

WestBow Press
A Division of Thomas Nelson & Zondervan
1663 Liberty Drive
Bloomington, IN 47403
www.westbowpress.com
1 (866) 928-1240

ISBN: 978-1-9736-8278-3 (sc)
ISBN: 978-1-9736-8277-6 (e)

Print information available on the last page.

WestBow Press rev. date: 12/23/2019

PREFACE

I am writing this book because the Bible speaks about books in the book of Ecclesiastes. And further, by these, my son, be admonished: of making many books there is no end; and much study is weariness of the flesh. Eccl. 12:12. And many other signs truly did Jesus in the presence of his disciples, which are not written in this book: John 20:31.

Handbook, children's or juvenile book, atlas, cookbook, guide book, storybook, songbook, tradebook, reference book, fiction, nonfiction, textbook, workbook, hymnbook, bible or Bible, treatise, libretto, tract, thesis, portfolio, album, dissertation. A division of a literary composition, chapter, record, register, roster, An account of transaction, call to account, list.

Kinds of books: 1. bring to book—reprimand, call to account, test see examine. 2. by the book—according to the rules, properly, correctly: see accurately, well. 3. in one's book — in one's opinion, for oneself, to one's mind, see personally 4. in one's good book (s) — liked, favored, approved: see honored. 5. in the good book— practiced, done, established, prevalent, see known.

6. know like a book— understand, comprehend, be aware of; see know. 7. make (a) book—bet, risk, aeger, see gamble 8. one for the books— source of amazement, shock, novelty, see surprise. 9. on the books—listed, noted, set down, see recorded. 10. throw the book at—the maximum punishment, charge with possible offense, be overzealous with; see accuse.

11. book—charge, take into custody, prefer charges; see accuse, arrest. 12. bookcase—bookshelf, cabinet, sectional bookcase, secretary, see also furniture. 13. booked—(Schedule)—engaged, contracted, due, obligated, billed, advertised; see also proposed (Arrested) —charged, taken into custody, jailed; see accused, under arrest. 14. bookish—scholarly, academic, erudite; see learned. 15. bookeeper— controller or comptroller, actuary, auditor; see accountant, clerk. 16. booking—accountancy, auditing, recording, accounting. 17. book review—critical review, notice, blurb, see review. 18. bookworm—savant, book lover, bibliophile (book lover, reader, bibliolater, antquarian, bibliomantic,, book nut.

This is not just another book but it is a book inspired by God to write to the Body of Baptized Believers of Jesus Christ Our Lord and Saviour concerning God's Divine Alignment for his Divine Assignment the Pulpit according to the book of Isaiah, For my thoughts are not your thoughts, neither are your ways my ways, saith the Lord. For as the heavens are higher than the earth, so are my ways higher than your ways, and my thoughts than your thoughts (Isaiah 55:8-9) Michael Day's personal commentary is God's thoughts is more intellent than our thoughts.

A pastor must love Pastoring more than he love Preaching, Pastoring is Shepherding the sheeps pastor is a gift to the body of Christ/Church (Eph. 4:11).

Preaching is a Calling (Matt. 4:18-22). The pulpit commitee does not Appoint Pastors to God's pulpit. The pastor is also the church administrator and he is responsible for every details of the local assembly God's has align and assign him for an indefinite period of time.

And they "Appointed" two, Joseph called Barsabas, who was surnamed Justus, and Matthias. And they prayed, and said, Thou, Lord, which knowest the hearts of all men, shew whether these two thou hast chosen. That he may take part of this ministry and apostleship, which Judas by transgression fell, that he might go to his own place. And they gave forth their lots: (vote) and the lot fell upon Matthias; and he was numbered with the eleven apostles. (Acts 1:23-26).

The purpose of this book is remind us of things we already know and make us aware of some non-biblical terms the scriptures does not support. This book was written both from a African-American perspective as well as Caucasions.

WIKIPEDIA Resource: on youtude on cell phone 12/13/18 make mention the term in the bible "Man of God" title 78 times in 72 verses of the bible, in application to up to 13 individuals title of respect applied to prophets and beloved religious leaders. There is no biblical term "Woman" of God this title is man-made title to try make woman equal with "The Man of God." Question is women is equal with men? Man of God is the description given to a man that follows God in every way, who obeys his command with joy (2 Tim. 3:17) (Josh. 24:15)

ACKNOWLEDGMENTS

I would like to acknowledge my lovely wife of more than 30 years, Vanessa, to whom this book is dedicated. Through you I have learned so many valuable lessons about life and love. Thank you for 30 years of ministry and fulfillment.

I would like to thank my pastor and his wife David and Doris Perry for 37 years of dedicated service at the Bethlehem No. 1 Missionary Baptist Church. Mercer, Tn.

I also must thank my brother and his wife Charlie and Geneva Day for encouragement to write this book.

I am thankful for pastor Willie and Doris Miles of the Sign of the Dove Ministry Jackson, Tn. for their loyal support and words of encouragements.

I also want to acknowledge Patricia Taylor secretary of Bethlehem No. 1 Church for words of encouragements to write this book.

I would like to thank my long time friend and colleague and mentor in ministry Dennis E. Blalock pastor of the New St. Luke Missionary Baptist Church in Jackson, Tn.

I also thank my editor Mrs. Linda Rainer of the St. Paul Missionary Baptist Church Medon, Tn.

And I would like to thank my chief editor Ernest Easely First Baptist Missionary Church in Cleveland, Tn.

INTRODUCTION

This book is written as a inspiration and insight to the body of Christ for quality leadership purposes and bring about a greater awareness of the relationship between the pulpit and the pew. I feel like a pastor must love pastoring as well as preaching one can preach without pastoring but one cannot pastor without preaching.

Because of my past 21 years of pastorialship experiences of untrained pulpit and untrained pew has been a hinder to the body of Christ. The ultimate trainer of the congregation is in the personality of the Holy Spirit. Only when the pulpit/pastor and pew/member spend adequately time daily with the influence and guidance of the Holy Spirit will bring glory to the kingdom of God (Jn. 14:26).

Sometimes it seem as though God himself has problems finding a man to fill this divine assignment (Jer. 3:15; Jer. 5:1; Ezek. 22:30). Through observation and conversation with the pulpiteer and pew member many has the mindset like the church belong to them. Sometimes degrees don't always make good leadership. The model church preachers/apostles relied on God and the Holy Spirit rather than resumes, degrees, newspaper, social media and other resources to fill God's divine assignment.

For it is written in the book of Psalms, Let his habitation be desolate, and let no man therein: and his bishoprick let another take. Wherefore of these men which have companied with us all the time that the Lord Jesus went in and out among us. Beginning from the baptism of John, unto that same day that he was taken up from us, must one be ordained to be a witness with us of his resurrection. And they appointed two, Joseph called Barsabas, who was surnamed Justus, and Matthias. "And they prayed", and said, "Thou, Lord, which knowest the hearts of all men, shew us whether of these two thou hast chosen". That he may take part of this ministry and apostleship, from which Judas by transgression fell, that he might go to his own place. And they gave forth their lots: and the lot fell upon Matthias: and he was numbered with the eleven apostles (Acts 1:20-26).

Sometimes we like to take short cuts with God by not taking adequately time in personal and corporate prayers for this matter. The must of the matter is to be Christ-minded, mission-minded, and kingdom minded, team-minded to reach the lost. Without a shepherd sheeps scatters (Jn. 10:1-18).

Through observation prayers is not a prority in the life of the body of baptized believers of Jesus Christ until some kind of crisis happen. There ought to be much prayers and supplications (Lk. 18:1; Phil. 4:6; 1 Thess. 5:17). Calling a pastor to vacant pulpit is and can be very challenging and discouragement through the process of it all.

There has not been enough teaching and training of the Holy Spirit's way of operating in the body of Christ. "The Greater Intimacy" of the pulpit and pew the greater the discernment of making the right choice of leadership (Pr. 3:5-6; Jer. 10:23; Jas. 4:8; Jas. 5:16; Isa. 55:8).

Calling a pastor is one of the most difficult thing to do in this 21st century. It is a risky business like everything else there is a urgency for all members of the body of Christ to pray for there sister church when they are without a pastor. Going days, weeks, months, and sometimes years without a pastor can be a unhealthy church (Eph. 4:27).

For the time will come when they will not endure sound doctrine: but after their own lusts shall they heap to themselves teachers, having itching ears (2 Tim. 4:3). Sometimes poor quality structure and leadership training is the down fall of our homes, churches, and community and the church is not fulfilling the great commission of making disciples of Jesus Christ (Matt. 28:18-20). MEN OUGHT ALWAYS PRAY (Lk. 18:1).

Divine mean dedicated to the service of God. Hallowed, sacred, devotional, spiritual, sacrificial, consecrated, anointed, ordained, sanctified, scriptural,, blessed, prayerful, reverenced, faithful, ministerial, worshipful. y gy

THE ROLE OF THE FIRST LADY

OR

THE PASTOR'S WIFE

The term First Lady is not in the bible. The term Elect Lady is in the bible. The elder unto the elect lady and her children...(2 John 1:1, 13) the person or church to which 2 John is addresed.

Elect mean a person or group choesn by God for special favor and for the rendering of special service to Him.

In the Old Testament the Hebrew people were described as God's elect. The New Testament speaks of Christ as God's Chosen One (1 Pet. 2:4, 6) and of the church as God's new chosen people (Rom. 8:33).

I don't want to spend a lot of time on the history of this passage you are welcome to do your own research if it's imporant to you. My reason to addressed this subject because our role in the home has a lot to do with biblical doctrine verses our man-made theology and our culture is destroying not only our home/family and our churches.

This term First Lady could derived from our Presidents of the United States of America wife term as First Lady. When God divinely appoint or assigned a pastor to a congregation as Overseer (Acts 20:28) sometimes in the past and even now the pastor's wife conduct and character has cause him to lose churches. When God calls a pastor to oversee a congregation the pastors role is not the same as his wife. (For if a man know not how to rule his own house, how shall he take care of the church of God (1 Tim. 3:5).

I do believe all First Ladies has to have a special anointing and calling (salvation) on her life to be able to perform her role as First Lady and be submissive to God as well as her husband.

There is no term in the bible "CO-PASTOR" when we study the leadership style of Jesus he did not labour his disciples/apostles as Co-Pastor many people seems to be more title-minded than biblical or Christ minded. For we are labourers together with God...(1 Cor. 3:9). The title of Adam wife was "help meet"...I will make him an "help meet" for him (Gen. 2:18). The pastor's wife is a "help meet" to him not co-pastor. It is very important for First Ladies conduct themselves because they are representative of the first family of the church and the kingdom of God.

Let your light so shine before men, that they may see your good works, and glorify your Father which is in heaven (Matt. 5:16). God has never assigned two pastors to one church (Jer. 3:15).

ROOT OF THE PROBLEM

IN

CHURCH LEADERSHIP

When you spend more time with God you act like Him.

When you spend more time with satan you act like him.

When you spend more time with yourself you act like yourself.

When you spend more time with other people you act like other people. This is called "Influence."

Some church marquee' read what's missing in the church UR. UR is not missing in the church it's "PRAYER" is what's missing in the church/body of Christ. Lk. 18:1; Heb. 10:25; Mk. 1:35. There's always people in the church and at the church but they're not always at "PRAYER" meetings. Many people use "Prayer" as a spare tire only when needed.

The Bible has sugar diabetes because many in the body of Christ has "Sugar Coated" the scriptures and the gospel of Jesus Christ. The pulpit continue to preach and teach feel-good sermons and this not a healthy church. Diabete is a disorder gland in our bodies the body of Christ doctrine and fellowship is out of order (1 Cor. 14:33, 40).

All and some Denominations/religious groups/belief/ has called the body of Christ a church without Biblical doctrines (1 Cor. 1:10; Eph. 4:4-6; Matt. 16:18).

There are more untrained leaders in the pulpit today than ever before with P.H.D degrees, Doctor of Divinity, Theological Seminary Training, etc. The term senior pastor is not in the bible. P.H.D. can mean spiritual "Post Hole Diggers" without proper leadership training untrained leaders can digged holes in the ministry and this can be the leading cause of church burnouts and pastors short tenures and revolving doors of all denominations.

Is there such thing a man can master God divinity and not able to master God's pulpit. I've known pastors that pastor seven churches with credentials. I refuse to attend a non-structure congregation who has poor quality praise and worship services like I have in the past. It is awful to hold services over certain lenght of time and you wonder why the Lord is not adding to that congregation people is not going to tell you they won't be back they show you they won't be back by not coming back (1 Cor. 14:40).

There is no passages of scripture in the bible that a pastor has to have the church to vote a deacon off the board for poor job performance. Untrained, unsaved, undevoted, un-born again, unconcerned, undedicated, unforgiven, lazy, procrastinator, no tither, no Sunday School student, no Bible Study student can be like D-CON rat poison kill the ministry. Pastors has the right to dismissed any leader who has a history of poor job performance according to scriptures (1 Cor. 4:2; ...who we may appoint over this business Acts 6:3; Gal. 6:1).

Tradition deacons are unlike the biblical deacons full of the Holy Spirit. The Holy Spirit has never told any deacon to fight their spiritual leader any body who fight against their pastor is giving evidence you are not "saved." Those seven men did not fight those apostle... And all that believed were together, and had all things common (Acts 2:44). None of Jesus aposltes or leadership team fought against him. None of Moses leadership team fought against him (Ex. 18:13-27; Nu. 11:14-16).

WINSTON CHURCHHILL
"QUOTE"

Whatever you do in life.

Never give up

Never give up

Never give up

Never give up

plause!

Never give up

...be not weary in well doing. 1 Thess. 3:13

...And let us not be weary in well doing: Gal. 6:9

PASTOR AND TWO CHURCHES

There is no where in the scripture God assigned two churches to one pastor.

No man can served two masters: for either he will hate the one, and love the other; or else he will hold to the one, and despise the other. Ye cannot serve God and mammon (Matt. 6:24)

Nelson's New Illustrated Bible Dictionary: Ronald F. Youngblood and F.F. Bruce & R.K. Harrison definition of mammon is (riches, wealth, money, gold, material possessions) Some pastors security is wealth (see Jesus parable (Lk. 12:13-21) "For what is a man profit if he gains the whole world, and loses his own soul?" (Matt. 16:26; Mk. 8:36; Lk. 9:25)

We can think God speak to us about anything and not be his voice: Draw nigh to God, and he will draw nigh to you (...Jas. 4:8) Voices some times heard can be the voices of: God, satan, our own voice, and other people voices.

Author: Keith Harrell said in his book "Attitude Is Everything. Man voice can be louder than God's voice. Michael Day's personal commentary we can listen to the voices of: Greed, Need, Seed. This type of ministry of a pastor can cause burnouts (over commitment)

Voice of greed is having the wrong motive of ministry.

Voice of need is always feel like we need something. Voice of seed (tithes) never pay tithes, robbed God (Mal. 3:8-10)

Serving two churches can be greed one of the churches is use as a partime job.

JOB DESCRIPTIONS OF OFFICERS IN THE BODY CHRIST

And he gave some, apostles: and some, prophets: and some,
evangelist: and some, pastors and teachers. Ehpesians 4:11

1. Apostles—a special messenger of Jesus Christ; a person to whom Jesus delegated authority fo certain tasks. The word "apostle" is used of those twelve disciples whom Jesus sent out, two by two, during His ministry in Galilee to expand His own ministry of preaching and healing. It was on that occasion, evidently, that they were first called "apostles." (Mk. 3:14; 6:30; Lk. 6:12-13; Matt. 10:2-4; Acts 1:13-14). What was they called to do? Preach the gospel of Jesus Christ. Messengers.

2. Prophets—A person who spoke for God and who communicated God's message courageously to God's Chosen People—the nation of Israel.

The Prophet's Call. Prohets received their call or appointment directly from God. Some prohets, like Jeremiah or John the Baptist, were called before birth (Jer. 1:5; Lk. 1:13-16). Except for God's call, prophets had no special qualifications. They appeared from all walks of life. They included sheepbreeders and farmers like Amos (Amos 7:14).

Prophets sometimes became quite dramatic and acted out their messages. Isaiah went naked and barefoot for three years (Isaiah 20:2-3). Ezekiel lay on his left side for 390 days and on his right side for 40 more (Ezek. 4:1-8). In rare circumstances, God used the hesitant or unruly to bear his message. Balaam prophesied (Num. 22:6-24:24). Saul was not in fellowship with God when he prophesied (1 Sam. 10:23-24).

Some prohets were called for a lifetime. But sometimes prophets spoke briefly and no more (Num. 11:25-26). In either case, a prohet spoke with the authority of the Holy Spirit (Num. 11:29; 24:24). Jesus reference to Himself as a prophet in John 12:49-50 rests upon this standard of faithfully repeating God's word to people.

The main role of the prophet was to bear God's word for the purposes of teaching, reproving, correcting, and training in righteousness (2 Tim. 3:16). Prophets were referred to as messengers of the Lord (Isa. 44:26); (Hag. 1:13), servants of God (Amos 3:7) shepherds (Zech. 11:4, Jer. 17:16), and watchman (Isa. 62:6).

Following the entrance of the Hebrew people into the land of Canaan, many prophets appeared throughout Israel's history to aid and protect the nation. Most of the prophet was unidentified because they never wrote down their message. The prophets task required face-to-face confrontations and a spoken rather than a written message. Many times the prophet stood alone and spoke to an unsysympathic audience. Great courage and indepedence of spirit was required.

The first prophet mention after Joshua is unamed Judges (6:7-10). Prophets were to exact God's word and not seek their own glory. This unknown prophet appeared in the times of Gidion when Israel was falling back into idolatry. Rather than speak of the future, he called Israel to remember the Lord who delivered them from Egypt.

The next prophet was Samuel, whose vocation was from most of his youth (Sam. 7:15). Samuel provided a model for other prophets to follow (1 Sam. 19:20). Isaiah's 1:1 says that Isaiah ministry spanned four kings from the death of Uzziah (Isa. 6:1). These prophets in Joshua, Judges, 1 and 2 Samuel, and 1 and 2 Kings provided those books with the name of Former Prophets in the Hebrew canon. They actually overlapped in time the "latter" or "writing" prophets, known commomly as the major and minor prophets.

The Former Prophets dealt more with daily problems and the currents state of affairs, while the latter prophets wrote down for latter generation what would happen in the future. The writing prophets do not appear to be in chronological order, but they provide clues that can be matched with historical facts that suggest teir proper sequence.

Malachi faces problems such as priestly carelessness (Mal. 1:6-2:9), intermarriage with foreigners (Mal. 2:10-3:6), and "lack of tithing" (Mal. 3:7-4:3).

Prophetess—a female prophet. First Corthians 11:5 assumes the female role in prophesying, seen again in Philip's four virgin daughters (Acts 21:9). Other prophetesses such as Noadiah gained a bad reputation (Neh. 6:14).

3. Evangelist—a person authorized to proclaim the gospel of Christ (Male or Female). Literally, however, the word means, "one who proclaims good tidings" (Ehp. 4:11; 2 Tim. 4:5). The evangelist was a gift of God to the early church (Eph. 4:11). The evangelist were not attached to any specific local church. They travel over a wide geographical area, preaching to those to whom the Holy Spirit led them. The early disciples were also called evangelists (Acts 8:4)

All Christians today may continue the witness of the early evangelists. As they spoke and wrote of Jesus, so may Christians bring His message to others.

4. Pastor—the feeder, protector, and guide, or shepherd, of a flock of God's people in the New Testament times. In speaking of spiritual gifts, the apostle Paul wrote that Christ "gave some to be apostles, some prophets, some evangelist, and some pastors and teachers" (Eph. 4:11). The term "pastors" by this time in church history had not yet become an official title. The term implied the nourishing of and caring for God's people.

The Greek word translated "pastors" in Ephesians 4:11 is used in the New Testament of sheepherds, literally or symbolically (Matt. 25:32); of Jesus, the Good Shepherd (John 10); and of shepherds, "or leaders, of the church (Eph. 4:11). The NKJV uses the word "pastors" only in this verse. Also compare Jeremiah 23:1-2 (KJV).

5. Teacher—the act of instructing students or imparting knowlegde and information. As in the New Testament, the concept of teaching usually means instruction in the faith. Thus, teaching is to be distinguished from preaching, or the proclamation of the gospel to the non-Christian world. Teaching in the Christian world faith was validated by Jesus, who was called "Teacher" more than anything else.

Since sound instruction in the faith is essential to the spiritual growth of the Christians and to the development of the church, the Bible contains numerous passages that deal with teaching (Matt. 4:23; Luke 4:14; Acts 13:1-3; Rom. 12:6-8; Gal. 6:6)

Special attention is directed to the danger of false teachings. Christians are warned to test those who pervert (corrupt) the true gospel (2 Tim. 3:1-7; 1 peter 2:1-3). Sound teaching was a concept deeply engrained in the Jewish mind since Old Teatament times. Moses and Aaron were considered teachers of God's commandments (Ex. 18:20). Parents were also directed to teach their children about God and His statutes (Deut. 4:9-10).

6. Bishop— an overseer, elder, or pastor charge with the responsibility of spiritual leadreship in a local church in the New Testament. In the New Testament, Jesus is called the Bishop or "Overseer" of your souls" (1 Peter 2:25) In this passage the word is associated with the term shepherd. Their responsibility, given by the Holy Spirit, was to shepherd the church of God (Acts 20:28)

7. Deacon—a servant or minister; an ordained lay officer in many Christian churches. The term "deacon" occurs in only two passages in the NKJV (Phil. 1:1; 1 Tim. 3:8-13) In The Greek world, diakonos is translated as "servant" rather than "deacon." Diakonos was used to describe the work of a servant—a person who waited on tables or ministered as a religious official.

When the office of a deacon was established in the New Testament church it may have paralled the function of the Jewish synagogue assistant—an official who took care of the administrative needs of the assembly.

The origin of the office of deacon is usually related to the events desribe in Acts 6:1-6. The young Christian church in Jerusalem was experiencing growing pains, and it had become increasingly difficult for the apostles to distribute chartiable gifts to its needy members without neglecting their ministry of prayer and preaching.

The widows of the Greek or Gentile background complained to the apostles that they were not getting their just share of food and money. To meet this critical need, seven men erew chosen by the congregation and presented to the apostles (Acts 6:1-6). Although these men were not called deacons at that time, the Greek word used to decsribe their work comes from the same Greek root word.

While these "table servers" were appointed to receive an emergency and their assignment may sound somewhat common, these men possessed the very highest moral and spiritual credentials. They are described as "men of good reputation," full of the Holy Spirit and wisdom" (Acts 6:3). They were formally installed or commissioned in a service of prayer and the Laying of The Hands by the apostles (Acts 6:6)—a practice regarded as the scriptural precedent for the ordination of deacons as church officials.

As a result of the selection of these seven men, harmony was restored in the congregation and the church continued to grow in number and spirit (Acts 6:5, 7). The later evangelistic work of two of these original "deacons" Stephen and Philip, serves as a role model for the spiritual ministry of deacons today. The list of qualifications for deacons given in 1 Timothy 3 shows the this servant of the church was to be equipped for a spiritual ministry to serve with the bishop or pastor: "Likewise decons must be reverent, not double-tongue, not given to much wine, not greedy for money, holding the mystery of the faith with a pure conscience. But let these first be proved; then let them serve as deacons, being found blameless" (1 Tim. 3:8-10).

The deacon was expected to have an example home life (1 Tim. 3:11, 12), to be a proven leader, and possess flawless character. The work of Stephen and Philip strongly suggest that gifted deacons became a permanent part of the church's outreach to the world very early in its history. The thrilling activities of thes servants of the church sound much like the work of traveling evangelist, missionary, or lay preacher. Stephen is desribe as a man "full of faith and power" who "did great wonders and sgns among the people" (Acts 6:8). So convincing were his words and miracles that "they were not able to resist the wisdom and Spirit by which he spoke" (Acts 6:10).

While some responded in faith, Stephen's zeal for Christ stirred up powerful enemies (Acts 6:11-13). Bravely, by false witnesses, Stephen glorified the Lord even as he was put to death for his convictions (Acts 7:59-60). Philip was also an evangelist who "preached the things concerning the kingdom of God and the name of Jesus Christ" (Acts 8:9-13). After preaching to eager crowds in Samaria, Philip witnessed to a solitary Ethiopian in the desert and baptized him (Acts 8:26-38).

In the early years of the church, a difference of opinion arose about the role of deacons. Some church officials argued that no spiritual function had been assigned to deacons. But others insisted that deacons were a vital part of a church's ministry, with official duties to perform. Through the centuries deacons generally have serve as assistants to the clergy in the service of the sanctuary.

In the modern church deacons exist as a distinct "lower order of the clergy" in the Roman Catholic, Church of England, Episcopal, United Methodist, and other ritual churches. In other denominations, including Baptist, Prebysterian, and Congregation, deacons are lay people, sometimes ordained, who carry out variety of practical and spiritual ministries that assist the pastor. Deacons are often given administrative and financial duties, such as reviewing budgets and recommending new church programs.

In some churches, each deacon is assigned "spiritual" oversight of several families in the church. The deacon keeps close touch with the families in his charge to make certain they are involved in church life and are ministered to promptly at times of special need.

Paul wrote that the reward for faithfulness in the office of deacon is that they "obtain for themselves a good standing anf great boldness in the faith which is in Christ Jesus" (1 Tim. 3:13). The selfless deacon may also feel close kinship with his Master, who walked the earth as "One who serves" (Luke 22:27). According to Jesus, the true heroes in the kingdom of God are those who assume the role of diakonos a servant (Matt. 20:26).

JOB DESCRIPTION OF OFFICERS IN THE BODY

OF

CHRIST

CONTINUE

Deaconess—a female believer serving in the office of DEACON in a church.

The only New Testament reference to deaconess as a church office is Paul's description of Phoebe as a deaconess of the church in Cenchrea (Rom. 16:1).

The office of deaconess became a regular future organization as early as the first part of the second century. In A.D. 112, Pliny the Younger, governor of Bithynia, wrote a letter to the emperor Trajan on Rome, indicating that investination of Christians he had tortured two Christian maiden who were called deaconess.

The office of deaconess in the Eastern Church continued down to the 12th century. The widows of clergymen, who were not permitted to remarry, often served as deaconess. Some scholars believe that Paul's standards for widows in 1 Tim. 5:9-12 were applied to these deaconess.

There is no qualifications for the office of deaconess are specifically given in the New Testament. Traditon required deaconess to have mercy for people. There is no account of deaconess ordination in the Bible. In the United States the office of deaconess is most prominent today among Lutherans, Episcopalians, United Methodist, Presbyterians, Baptist.

In the early centuries, deaconess were especially called on to serve women in situations where custom did not allow the ministry of the deacon.

Deaconess instructed female candidates for church membership, ministered to women who were sick and in prison, and assisted at their baptism.

Through the years deaconess have been assigned various types of educational, chartiable, and social service work in their churches. They may be seen frequently today as ushers and lay readers.

SHEPHERD MINISTRY

FOR

HARDSHIP/EMERGENCY FUNDS

FOR CLERGYMEN AND WIVES

The clergymen of every city or town they pastor should have a Shepherd Ministry for Hardship Emergency Fund For Clergymen and their wives. S.M.H.E.F.C.W.

A pastor tenure can be 1. Terminated 2. Health Issue 3. Resigned 4. Retire 5. Death. My convictions is pastors ought not take better care of guest pastors or speakers out of town better than those in town to conduct revivals, leadership conferences, seminars, workshops, etc.

When pastors has to resigned because of some kind of conflicts in the church, or health issue, and retire, and, terminated, or pass a way, resigned. We sometimes experience financial instability during a crisis. The shepherd ministry can be a good benefit for our fallen "BROTHERS IN MINISTRY."

I have a good friend of mine testified he was a member of the shepherd ministry (Pastor) 400 membership strong bless him $ 20,000.00 for his hospital bill when he was hopitalized without any health insurance. This Emergency Fund can be a blessing to the pastors wives in the event he pass a way before she do. The "BUDGET" ought to consist of all churches in the "Network" allow money to be paid into this sheperd ministry.

Example: $ 100.00/ mo. x 12 mo. = $1,200 yr. x 5 yrs. = $ 6,000.00. $ 6,000 x 5 yrs. = $ 30,000.00. Even for all former pastors/associate ministers make some personal financial contributions to the shepherd ministry toward your "Rainy Day" and your "Unexpected Emergency" Day. The Pastors Is The Best Investment On The Face of the Earth. Pastors I have a serious problem with you abandoned our former pastors with some difficulty in their finances and you take better care of out of town pastors with flight, motel, food.

I was on a committee of a city-wide revival and we gave the guest speaker over $ 3,000.00 honoraium for three nights, plus flight, motel, food, $ 600.00 honoraium to a pastor to transport him (speaker) from his motel, Airport, Restaurant, $ 100.00 honoraium to those served on the committee then beg members to pay an assessment to finance the events.

All ye beasts of the field, come to devour; yea, all ye beasts in the forest. His watchmen are blind: they are all ignorant, they are all dumb dogs, they cannot bark: (preach) sleeping, lying down, loving to slumber. Yea, they are "greedy dogs" which can never have enough, and they "shepherds" that cannot understand: they all look their own way, every one for his gain, from his quarter (Isa. 56:9-11)

I know a church paid out over $ 3,000.00 to bury non-functioning church member got shot down in cold blood without any life insurance.

Jesus said unto him, Let the dead bury their dead...(Lk. 9:60)

For I have given them the words which thou gavest me; and they have received them, and have known surely I came out from thee, and they have believed that thou didst send me (John 17:8) I pray for them: "I pray not for the world (...John 17:9)"

As we have therefore opportunity, let us do good to all men, (especially unto them who are of the household of faith) (Gal. 6:10)

Adam Clark Commentary on the Bible Abridged By Ralph Earle:

(Isa. 56:11) Greedy dogs. Insatiably feeding themselves with fat, and clothing themselves with the wool, while the flock is scattered, ravaged, and starved.

Sometimes we say we don't know or we didn't know about our fellow clergymen crisis what about times you did know. What's First Lady is going to do when we have nothing for them to fall back on after we have pass a way. Pastors if you and your church has seven annual days a year you pay your guest preacher $ 100.00 x 7 $ 700.00 yr. Invest that money in your Shepherd Emergency Fund all our RAINY DAY'S is coming sooner or later.

Review the Scriptures for Shepherd Ministry:

Remember our fallen clergymen in times of crisis. Sometimes pastors have no life insurance even to have a decent burial.

The purpose of Shepherd Ministry is to give Pastors and First Lady some breathing room to pay off some "Priortized Major Bills" when face with "HARDSHIP."

I personally feel every guest speaker should be compensated well as well as our fallen clergymen.

HARDSHIPS/EMERGENCY/FUNDS/ SUPPORTING SCRIPTURES

FOR THE CLERGYMEN AND WIVES:

1. But whoso hath this world's good, and seeth his brother have need, and shutteth up his bowels of compassion from him, how dwelleth (live) the love of God in him. "compassion" webster dictionary mean "sympathy, consideration, kindness, pity" 1 John 3:17.

2. Withhold not good from them to whom it is due, when it is in thine hand to do it. Pr. 3:27

3. We then that are strong ought to bear the infirmities of the weak, and not to please ourselves. Romans 15:1 Webster-infirmities mean weakness, confinement, sickness, illness.

4. Let "brotherly love" continue. Hebrew 13:1 Webster-continue mean to keep it up.

5. Without "Faith" it is impossible to please him: for he that cometh to God must believe that he is, and that he is a rewarder to them that diligently seek him. Hebrew 11:6 Webster-diligently/diligence mean hardworking, alertness, intentness, attention, care. —ant. carelessness, laziness sloth.

6. Now therefore thus saith the Lord of host; Consider your ways. Haggai 1:5

7. Bring ye all the tithes into the storehouse...saith the Lord of hosts, if I will open you the windows of heaven, and pour you out a blessing, that there shall not be room enough to receive it. Malachi 3:10

8. Give, and it shall be given unto you; good measure, pressed down, shaken together, and running over, shall men give into your bosom. For with the same measure that ye mete withal it shall be measure to you again. Lk. 6:38

9. Owe no man anything, but to "love" one another: for he that loveth another hath fulfilled the law. Ro. 13:8

10. A new commandment I give unto you, that ye love one another; as I have loved you, that ye also love one another. By this shall all men know that ye are my disciples, if ye have love one to another. John 13:34-35.

11. ....Thou shalt not muzzle the mouth of the ox that treadeth out the corn. Doth God take care for oxen. 1 Cor. 9:9

12. If we have sown unto you spiritual things, is it a great thing if we shall reap your carnal things? 1 Cor. 9:11

13. Honor widows that are widows indeed. 1 Tim. 5:3

14. Let the elders that rule well be counted worthy of double honour, especially they who labour in the word and doctrine. 1 Tim. 5:17

15. The steps of a good man is ordered by the Lord; and he delighted in his way. Ps. 37:23

16. Come now, let us reason together, saith the Lord....Isa. 1:18

17. Then shall he answer them, Verily I say unto you, Inasmuch as ye did it not to one of the least of these, ye did it not to me. And these shall go away into everlasting punishment: but the righteous into life eternal. Matt. 25:45-46

18. What doth it profit, my brethren, though a man say he hath faith, and have not works? can a man faith save him. Jas. 2:14

19. If a brother or a sister be naked, and destitute of daily food. Jas. 2:15

20. And one of you say unto them, Depart in peace, be ye warmed and filled: notwithstanding ye give them not those things which are needful to the body; what doth it profit. Jas. 2:16

21. Even so faith, if it hath not works, is dead, being alone. Jas. 2:17.

22. Yea, a man say, Thou hast faith, and I have works: shew me thy faith without thy works, and I will shew thee my faith by my works. Jas. 2:18

23. Thou believest there is one God: thou doest well: the devils also believe, and tremble. Jas. 2:19

24. Read: Jas. 3:1-12;...Out of the same mouth proceedeth blessing and cursing. My brethren, these things ought not so to be. Jas. 3:10

25. ....yet ye have not, because ye ask not. Jas. 4:2

26. Beloved, let us love one another: for love is of God: and every one that loveth is born of God, and knoweth God. 1 John 4:7

27. He that loveth not knoweth not God; for God is love. 1 John 4:8

28. Herein is love, not that we loved God, but that he loved us, and sent his son to be the propitiation for our sins. 1 John 4:10 "propitiation"—atonement mean satisfy, pay for, compensate

29. If a man say, I love God, and hateth his brother, he a liar: for he that lovest not his brother whom he hath seen, how can he love God whom he hath not seen? 1 John 4:20

30. Beloved, if God so loved us, we ought also to love one another. 1 John 4:11

31. No man hath seen God at any time. If we love one another, God dwelleth in us, and his love is prefected (mature) in us. 1 John 4:12

32. Love not the world, neither the things that are in the world. If any man love the world, the love of the Father is not in him. 1 John 2:15

33. For all that is in the world, the lust of the flesh, and the lust of the eyes, and the pride of life, is not of the Father, but is of the world. 1 John 2:16

34. And the world passeth away, and the lust thereof: but he that doeth the will of God abideth forever. 1 John 2:17

35. Be not deceived: God is not mocked: for whatsoever a man sowed, that shall he also reap. Galatians 6:7

36. And let us not be weary in well doing: for in due season we shall reap, if we faint not. Galatians 6:9

37. As we have therefore opportunity, let us do good to all men, especially unto them who are the household of faith. Galatians 6:10

38. Wherefore be ye not unwise, but understanding what the will of the Lord is. Ehp. 5:17

39. ....but be filled with the Spirit. Eph. 5:18

40. Examine yourselves, whether ye be in the faith; prove yourselves, how that Jesus Christ is in you, except ye be "reprobates"? (wicked, hellbound, transgressor, disgusted, rejected by the Lord, unregenerate, good for nothing. 2 Cor. 13:5

CALLING A PASTOR

Let us pray together

Heavenly Father,

You said, but what saith it? The word is nigh the, even in thy mouth, and in thy heart: that is the word of faith, which we preach: Ro. 10:9. Lord, you said in your word, so then faith cometh by hearing by the word of God. Ro. 10:17.

We pray that as we place our confidence in you O Lord and your word instead in our own ability to chose the pastor or leader as our overseer, forgive us for spending time dwelling on our plans and ideas and ways of doing things. O Lord send us a God kind of pastor one who we can trust and obey. We take you at your word and help us to rely on you for your divine assignment O Lord. In Jesus name. Amen.

CALLING A PASTOR

Let us pray together

Heavenly Father,

The bible says, Son of man, I have made thee a watchman unto the house of Israel: therefore hear the word at my mouth, and give them warning. Ezk. 3:17 O Lord help us to hear and obey your word and your warning. O Lord you said in your word, Ask, and it shall be given you; seek, and ye shall find; knock, and it shall be opened unto you. Matt. 7:7 O Lord, Bless us with a pastor with a good character of integrity. One who will be committed, dedicated, and devoted to our Lord and saviour Jesus Christ and to this church family. We believe you want us to be on one accord. We thank you in advance dear Lord. In Jesus name. Amen.

Heavenly Father,   Let us pray togeteher

O Lord you said in your word, I will give you pastors according to mine heart; which shall feed you with knowledge and understanding. Jer. 3:15. O Lord we pray the Holy Spirit will help us make the right choice. O Lord your word say, And all things, whatsoever ye shall ask in prayer, believing, ye shall receive. Matt. 21:22 O Lord prepare our hearts and minds and temperaments by acknowleging our sins and traditions that may hinder our relationship with our new leader.

In Jesus name. Amen

CALLING A PASTOR

Let us pray together

Heavenly Father,

O Lord your word said, Trust in the Lord with all thine heart; and lean not unto thine own understanding. In all thine ways acknowledge him, and he shall direct thy paths. We pray O Lord help us not to do our own choosing. Proverbs 3:5-6. Dear Lord, we pray you will give our leader and pastor the ability and discernnment to make wise choices to move the church forward. Eternal God your word said, The steps of a good man are ordered by the Lord: and he delighted in his way. Though he fall, he shall not be utterly cast down: for the Lord upholdeth him with his hand. Ps. 37:23-24 In Jesus name. Amen.

CALLING A PASTOR

Let us pray together

Heavenly Father,

Dear, Lord your word said, Take heed therefore unto yourselves, and to all the flock, over the which the Holy Ghost hath made you overseers, to feed the church of God, which he hath purchased with his own blood. Acts 20:28 Dear, Lord send us a overseer who will preach and teach sound doctrine and is a people person, we pray he will be Holy Spirit train so that he may train us to follow his leadership and give us the faith to receive sound doctrine and apply it to our hearts. O Lord you said, Obey them that have the rule over you, and submit yourselves: for they watch for your souls, as they that must give account, that they may do it with joy, and not with grief: for that is unprofitable for you. Heb. 13:17. Help us to do good and not to forget to communicate and make such sacrfices, God is well pleased. Heb. 13:16 Lord, you said, men ought to always to pray, and not to faint. Lk. 18:1 Help us not to forget to pray for our pastor and one another. In Jesus name. Amen.

CALLING A PASTOR

Let us pray together

Heavenly Father,

Dear, Lord you said, so when they had dined, Jesus said to Simon Peter, Simon, son of Jonas, lovest thou me more than these? He saith unto him, Yea, Lord; thou knowest that I love thee. He saith unto him, Feed my lambs. He saith unto him again the second time, Simon son of Jonas, lovest thou me? He saith unto him, Yea, Lord; thou knowest that I love thee. He saith unto him, Feed my sheep. He saith unto him the third time, Simon, son of Jonas, lovest thou me? Peter was grieved because he saith unto him the third time, Lovest thou me? And he said unto him, Lord, thou knowest all things; thou knowest that I love thee, Jesus saith unto him, Feed my sheep. O Lord, we pray your word to you because we know you honor your word. In Jesus name. Amen.

CALLING A PASTOR

Let us pray together

Heavenly Father,

O Lord your word said,trust in the Lord with all thine heart; and lean not unto thine own understanding. In all thy ways acknowledge him, and he shall direct thy paths. Pr. 3:5-6 We

"PRAY" O Lord, help us not to do our own choosing. Dear Lord, we pray you will bless our leader and pastor the ability to discerned to make good decisions that will benefit the kingdom God and move the church forward.

Lord you said, the steps of a good man is ordered by the Lord; and he delighted in his way. though he fall, he shall not be utterly cast down: for the Lord upholdeth him with his hand. Psalm 37:23. In the name of "JESUS." Amen.

O Lord you said, Verily, verily, I say unto you, He that entereth not by the door into the sheepfold, but climbeth up some other way, the same is a thief and a robber. But he that entereth in by the door is the sherpherd of the sheep. To him the porter openeth: and the sheep hear his voice: and he calleth his own sheep by name, and leadeth them out. And when he putteth forth his own shep, he goeth before them, and the sheep follow him: for they know his voice. And a stranger will they not follow, BUT WILL FLEE FROM HIM: for they know not the voice of strangers. John 10:1-5

Heavenly Father,

You said, Verily, verily, I say unto you, I am the door of the sheep. John 10:7..I am the good shepherd: the good shepherd giveth his life for the sheep. v.11. I am the good shepherd, and know my sheep, and am known of mine. v.14. I am the door: by me if any man enter in, he shall be saved, and shall go in and out, and find pasture. v.9 Dear Lord send us a "God-Sent" Shepherd to Shepherd us. In the name of "JESUS." Amen.

And other sheep I have, which are not of this fold: them also I must bring, and they shall hear my voice; and there shall be one fold, and one sherphed. v.16

Therefore doth my Father love me, because I lay down my life, that I might take it again. v.17

Model-Minded, Christ-Minded, Mission-Minded, Kingdom-Minded

Faith-Driven, Shred It!

Model-minded

To model is to imitate, duplicate, or to served as an example in the community. The New Testament church model the leadership style of Jesus Christ through The Acts of the Apostles chapter 2:41-47. They gladly received his word and were baptized some of today's churches is gladly receiving the word and is baptized but it seem as though the body of Christ is not continuing stedfast or faithful in the Sunday School, and Bible Study as well as other chrisian education activities v. 44 and all that believed were together, and had all things common v.46 and they, continuing daily with one accord in the temple (Heb. 10:25) The African-American church tradition mindset is v. 46 is to break bread during annual days which does not model the model church.

To be Christ-Minded (Phil. 2:5) is a mind to please his heavenly Father.

I can of mine own self do nothing: asl hear, I judge: and my judgment is just: because I seek not mine own will, but the will of the Father which hath sent me (Jn. 5:30). I received not honour from men (Jn. 5:41) At that day ye shall know that I am in my Father, and ye in me, and I in you (Jn. 14:20). Paul also and Barnabas continued in Antioch, teaching and preaching the word of the Lord, with many others also (Acts 15:35).

Mission-Minded: To be mission-minded is to know our purpose. Go ye therefore, and teach all nations, baptizing them in the name of the Father, and of the Son, and of the Holy

Ghost. Teaching them to observed all things whatsoever I have commanded you: and, lo, I am with you alway, even unto the end of the world (Matt. 28:19-20).

Kingdom-Minded: To be kingdom-minded is to seek the kingdom of God first and his righteousness: and all these things shall be added unto you (Matt. 6:33)

Faith-Purpose- Driven: Everything we do for the Lord must be to please God. Now faith is the substance of things hoped for, the evidence of things not seen. But without faith it is impossible to please him: for he that cometh to God must believe that he is, and that he is a rewarder of them that diligently seek him (Heb. 11:1, 6) Faith must drive us to our destiny.

Shred It: mean to tear, strip, cut into small pieces. There are some habits we must get rid of to call a pastor to an vacant pulpit. We must shred our tradition mindset by forgetting those things which are behind, and reaching forth unto those things which are before. I press toward the mark for the prize of the high calling of God in Christ Jesus (Phil. 3:13-14).

PRAYER AND LEADERSHIP

TRAINING

There has been some misconceptions, with the Deacon board/ministry and the church, with their cultural mindset, to think the pastor only is to pastor the people, and have nothing to do with the finances or money. The newly elected pastor should be informed of the financial status of the church after he has been elected. The pastor is the overseer of God's heritage, not only the people, but also, the money or finances, also the church property. "Take heed therefore unto yourselves, and to all the flock, over which the Holy Ghost hath made you overseers, to feed the church of God (not man) which he hath purchase with his own blood. Ac. 20:28".

1. Why Churches Die. Mac Brunson & Ergun Caner book, Why Churches Die? Speaks about the diagnosing Lethal (deadly poison) gossip, cause the church to die. But the tongue can no man tame: it is an unruly evil, full of deadly poison. Jas. 3:8. Many people in the body of Christ is immature in the faith, therefore, they are easy to be offended with what people say about them. The scriptures teaches us in the book of Phil. 2:14 Do all things without murmurings and disputings. Many people in the body of Christ is not trained by the Holy Spirit to control their tongue. People carry or harbor bitterness, anger, "Let no corrupt communication proceed out of your mouth, but that which is good to the use of edifying, that it may minister grace unto the hearers. Ehp. 4:29. The life of the Church is prayer, we must asked God in prayer, for the ablitiy to govern our attitude." Let all bitterness, wrath, and anger, and clamour, and evil speaking, be put away from you, with all malice: And be ye kind one to another, tenderhearted, forgiving one another, even as God for Christ sake hath forgiven you. Eph. 4:31-32.

2. Autopsy Of A Deceased Church. Thom S. Rainer, book, suggest, what are some of the reasons or causes of congregation/churches die? Churches never die, individual die, sometimes indvidual has to die for the church to live. Sometimes, pastors has to make many trips to the cemetery for those contrary members. Let's examined some of the causes of decline in church growth. 1. Short pastorial tenure. (2-5 yrs). 2. The church rarely prays together. 3. No zeal, or trained for evangelism. 4. No visions, 5. no faith, 6. not kingdom minded, 7. not want to spend money, 8. declined in midweek, prayer and bible study. 9. untrained pulpit, 10. untrained pew, 11. burnouts

3. What is A Healthy Church? Mark Dever, book, The process of calling a pastor is very important to God and to the community. I am thankful to be a member of a healthy church, The Bethlehem No. 1. Missionary Baptist Church 183 Maple Springs Rd. Mercer, Tn. Pastor David L. Perry, his tenure is 36 years. Pastor Perry has been and still is a visionary, his vision is for the church to a beacon to the community. Under the leadership of Pastor Perry, the church has grew from a membership of less than 50 members to over 1500 or more. The church grew rapidly we now enjoying our new building/sanctuary/mutlpurpose facilitiy.

Bethlehem is a healthy church, because of the leading, and guidance, of the Holy Spirit of our pastor providing us with persistent Leadership training. What contribute to a healthy church? 1. A praying church 2. Sound Doctrine 3. Youth Ministry 4. Children Ministry 5. Agape Love 6. Healthy Fellowship 7. Healthy Budget 8. Family Values 9. Unity 10. Compensate the Pastor Benefit Package. 11. Communication 12. Forgiving 13. Men 14. Commitment 15. Good Structure 16. Music Dept.

The process of calling a pastor to a vacant church, God's way. Through much unity prayers of the body of Christ. Praise the Lord, the Bethlehem church family has a property value, estimate of 3.5 million dollars. The Church Must Pray Together. Lk. 18:1.

4. The Must of the Matter. The Reverend Jerry D. Black, book, The Process of Calling A Pastor, we must pray, Calling a Pastor is a serious matter. "He must increase, but I must decrease. Jn. 3:30" "And he must needs go through samaria. Jn. 4:4" "God is Spirit: and they that worship him must worship him in spirit and in truth. "And brought them out, and said, Sirs, what must I do to be saved?" Ac. 16:30 "But without faith it is impossible to

please him: for he that cometh to God must believe that he is, and that he a rewarder of them tht diligently seek him. Heb. 11:6

FIRST LADIES BURNOUTS CAN CAUSE DROPOUTS

Sometimes when pastors take on leadership roles as shepherds or overseer of a congregation sometimes the role of the wife has to fulfilled can cause burnouts without good leadership structure and balance.

The First Lady is the only lady in the church has to share her husband with the whole congregation and with her husband duties and responsibilites somtimes can be very stressful and more than they were expecting or called to do. Here are some details in the role of First Lady: 1. Home/ Husband/Children(s)/ Grandchildren(s)/Family Affairs-Time/ Church Affairs/ Two Churches/ Large Churches/Job/Personal Affairs-Financial.

In my conversation with both former and present first-ladies has expressed to me they tried very hard to filled that role and as a result getting a divorced this is not a position in the church everyone can filled. Praise God for every pastor who has a God-Sent and Supportive wife in ministry. I personally thank God for my wife Venessa Day for our 30 yrs. of marriage, ministry, celebrate her job.

The bible is silent concerning first lady Moses during his ministry as to what role did she fulfilled (Ex. 2:21).

God told Jeremiah not to take a wife. The word of the Lord came also unto me, saying, Thou shalt not take a wife, neither shalt thou have sons or daughters in this place (Jere. 18:1-2). Because of the grievous deaths in the Land.

In the New Testament the bible give references of one disciple of Jesus being married. And when Jesus was come into Peter's house, he saw his wife's mother laid, and sick of a fever (Matt. 8:14). Theologians said most or all the apostles were married.

In the Old Testament Ezekiel wife died symbolizing the destruction of "dlight of the Jews' eyes", temple. Also the word of the Lord came unto me, saying, Son of man, behold, I take away from thee the desire of thine eyes with a stroke: yet neither shalt thou mourn nor weep, neither shall thy tears run down. Forbear to cry, make no mourning for the dead, bind the tire of thine head upon thee, and put on thy shoes upon thy feet, and cover not thy lips, and eat not the bread of men. So I spake unto the people in the morning: and even my wife died: and I did in the morning as I was commanded (Ez. 24:15-18). There is nothing wrong with first ladies experience this type of minstry life-style. If pastors and other leaders in the church go through this same situation we all can overcommit ourselves with burnouts that causes dropouts of marriages, church, organization, etc.

....It is enough: now, O Lord, take away my life: for I am not better than my fathers (1 Ki. 19:4)

SUPPORTING SCRIPTURES

FOR

PASTORS/DEACONS/MEN

King James Versions Bible

Pastors: Jeremiah 3:15; Ezekiel 3:16-17; Numbers 11:1-35;

Exodus 18:1-27; Jeremiah 29:11; Matthew 6:33; Matthew 7:7-7

1 Thessalonians 5:12-14; Hebrew 6:10; Hebrew 13:17; Ezekiel 22:30; Jeremiah 5:1; Hebrew 13:1; Acts 2:41-47; John 13:34-35

Only Two Biblical Offices In The Bible/Church/Congregation

Structure: Pastors/Deacons/Role/Relationship /Model Church

Deacons: Acts 6:1-15; 1 Timothy 3:1-16; Philippians 1:1

1 Corinthians 14:33, 40; Ephesians 4:1-32; Romans 10:1-17;

Romans 12:9-21; Romans 13:8; Romans 14:12; Romans 14:16-19

2 Corinthians 5:10; 17; 2 Thessalonians 3:6-7

1. Where did pastors originate? Who ordained pastors? (Jer. 1:5)

2. Where did deacons originate? Who ordained deacons/men? (Acts 6:6)

3. Who appointed deacons/men? (Acts 6:3)

4. Who chose the deacons /men? (Acts 6:2-3)

5. Why men/deacons were chosen? (Acts 6:1)

6. Who laid hands on these deacons/men? (Acts 6:6)

7. Why these seven deacons/men needed to be screened? (Acts 6:3)

9. Who was hurting or neglected in the daily ministration? (Acts 6:1) ministration mean assistance, help, support, aid.

10. Why it didn't make no sense for the 12 apostles to served tables? (Acts 6:2) reason mean intelligence, ability, judgment, resourceful, discerning, clear-headed, skill, having a head on one's shoulder, the mind or the power to reason.

11. The ultimate purpose (need) for the 12 apostles? (Acts 6:4)

12. What's the Problems With The Lord's Church In This 21st Century? It's not "UR" MISSING IN THE CHURCH BUT (PRAYER) IS MISSING IN THE CHURCH" "UR" AT THE CHURCH BUT NOT IN PRAYER.

13. The team concepts in Acts 6:1-7 had good results v.7.

14. This unified body of believers were pleased with their intelligent decision with chosen the twelve v.5.

15. The keys to Church Growth and Development is "Prayer" and "Unity" and "Christian Education" and "Salvation" "God the Father" "God the Son" and "God the Holy Spirit" "Equipment the Saints" with the "WORD" (John 1:1).

16. Key Verses For Prayer: ...but served God with fastings and prayers night and day (Lk. 2:37) ...Give us this day our daily bread (Matt. 6:11). ...he departed into a solitary (alone) place, and there prayed (Mk. 1:35) ...that men ought always to pray and not to faint (give

up) (Lk. 18:1) Pray without ceasing (1 Thess. 5:17) And this is life eternal, that they might know thee the only true God, and Jesus Christ, whom thou hast sent (John 17:3)

That they all may be one; as thou, Father, art in me, and I in thee, that they may be one in us: that the world may believe that thou hast sent me. And the glory which thou gavest me I have given them; that they may be one, even as we are one: ...that they may be made perfect in one: and that the world may know that thou hast sent me, and loved them, as thou hast loved me. Father, I will that they also, whom thou hast given me, be with me where I am; that they may behold my glory, which thou hast given me: for thou lovest me before the foundation of the world (John 17:21-24).

O righteous Father, the world hath not known thee: but I have known thee: but I have known thee, and these have known that thou hast sent me. And I have declared unto them thy name, and will declare it: that the love wherewith thou hast loved me may be in them, and I in them (John 17:25-26).

HOLY SPIRIT

THE ULTIMATE TRAINER

calling a pastor to a vacant pulpit

When calling a pastor to a vacant pulpit as leader and shepherd of the flock may already has seminary training and degrees. The ultimate trainer for leadership in the home, church, community is the Holy Spirit. He is our coach, school teacher or classroom teacher, supervisor, leadership instructor, our comforter.

But the Comforter, which is the Holy Ghost, whom the Father will send in my name, he shall teach you all things, and bring all things to your remembrance; whatsoever I have said unto you (John 14:16)

The Holy Spirit only can be our ultimate trainer when we spend quality time and intimacy with him daily as we seek his guidance in leadership.

Neverthelesss I tell you the truth: It is expedient for you that I go away: For if I go not away, the Comforter will not come unto you: but if I depart, I will send him unto you (John 16:7). He is our daily mind regulator and keep us in fellowship with our heavenly Father and he will never leave us nor forsake us ....I will never leave thee, nor forsake thee (Heb. 13:5).

Howbeit when the Spirit of truth, is come, he will guide you into all truth: for he shall not speak of himself: but whatsoever he shall hear, that shall he speak: and he will shew you things to come (John 16:13). The Holy Spirit is our guide. ...And he said, How can I, except some man should guide me?...(Acts 8:31). He's Holy Spirit Divine who make divine alignment for his divine assignment. He is our leader ...he leadeth me beside the still waters .... he leadeth me in the paths of righteousness for his name sake (Psa. 23:2, 3).

He said unto them, have ye received the Holy Ghost since ye believed? And they said unto him, We have not so much as heard whether there be any Holy Ghost (Acts 19:2) Jesus Christ was full of the Holy Spirit. The Spirit of the Lord is upon me, because he hath anointed me to preach the gospel to the poor: he hath sent me to heal the broken hearted, to preach deliverance to the captives, and recovering of the sight to the blind, to set at liberty them that are bruised. To preach the acceptable year of the Lord (Lk. 4:18-19).

The ultimate trainer the Holy Spirit when both the pulpit and the pew spend quality time with him he will have the power of influence in the congregation. Wherever we go, we must take your team spirit with you. Leaders should have a greater faith in God and keep a abundant mindset to always seek ways for progress and to keep a healthy self esteem. The Holy Spirit will train us to have a great faith. A leader is not going to very successful without faith.

But without faith it is impossible to please God....(Heb. 11:6).

....be of good comfort: thy faith hath made thee whole. (Matt. 9:22).

....O woman, great is thy faith (Matt. 15:28).

....Daughter, thy faith hath made thee whole...(Mk. 5:34).

....Have faith in God (Mk. 11:22).

....Where is your faith? (Lk. 8:25).

So then faith cometh by hearing, and hearing by the word of God (Ro. 10:17).

....Verily I say unto you. If ye have faith, and doubt not...(Matt. 21:21).

.....for whatsoever is not of faith is sin (Ro. 14:23).

(For we walk by faith, not by sight:) (2 Cor. 5:7).

Now faith is the substance of things hoped for, the evidence of things not seen (Heb. 11:1).

That the trial of your faith...(1 Pt. 1:7).

Knowing this, that the trying of your faith worketh patience (Jas. 1:3, 6)

What doth it profit, my brethren, though a man say he hath faith, and have not works? can a man faith save him? (Jas. 2:14). Even so faith, if it hath not works, is dead. being alone v.17 Yea, a man may say, Thou hast faith, and I have works: shew me thy faith without thy works, and I will shew thee my faith by my works, and I will shew thee my faith by my works v.18

When you become a leader there will be times when your faith will be tested sometimes worst than other times. Great leaders never desire to lead but serve. But ye, bloved, building up yourselves on your most holy faith, praying in the Holy Ghost. Keep yourselves in the love of God, looking for the mercy of our Lord Jesus Christ unto eternal life. And of some have compassion, making a difference. And others save with fear, pulling them out the fire: hating even the garment spotted by the flesh. Now unto him that is able to keep you from falling, and to present you from fautltless before the presence of his glory with exceeding joy. The only wise God our Saviour, be glory and majesty, dominion and power, both now and ever. Amen. (Jude 20-25).

The Holy Spirit who is the ultimate trainer has the mind of Christ (Phil. 2:5). A leader will seek ways to serve not to be served. But it shall not be so among you: but whoever will be great among you, let him be your minister: Even the Son of man came not to be ministered unto, but to minister, and to give his life a ransom for many (Matt. 20:26-28).

I have in my library a plaque says: Faith makes things possible not easy. I have another plaque in my garage says: The struggle is real but my faith is stronger. Sometimes things seems impossible until it's done and when it get hard to pray pray the hardest and have faith in God. Always remember today is a perfect day to start living your dreams and today is a good day to have a great day.

Stan Toler book Minute Motivators For leaders: Stan Toler says, Leaders don't have all the answers, though others may think they do. Stan Toler book: Leaders shoulders with great leaders. "Anyone who influences others is a leader" (chuck swindoll) every leader should be a mentor as well as have a mentor.

TERM USED

SUPPOSED TO BE A PREACHER

Many in the body of Christ used the terminology about one's character as preacher or pastor. It is only by the grace of God anyone tenure in the pulpit (Ro. 3:23). God always used unlikely people in ministry. Just to name a few:

1. Abraham- adultery, liar (Gn. 16:1-6; 20:2). (father of all nation)
2. Moses—murder (Ex. 2:5-14). Prophet
3. David—murder, adultery (King) (2 Ki. 11:1-27; 12:1-31).
4. Jonah—disobedience (Jonah 1:1-3). (prophet)
5. Peter—denies Jesus (Matt. 26:69-75). (disciple, apostle)
6. Thomas—doubts Jesus (Jn. 20:26-29). (disciple, apostle)
7. Judas Iscariot— betrayal of Jesus (Mk. 14:10-11). (disciple, apostle)
8. Pastors 21st century (Jer. 3:15; Jer. 5:1; Ezek. 22:30; Ro. 10:15; Acts 20:28).
9. Paul—persecutor, chief of sinners (Acts 9:1-9; 1 Tim. 1:15).

IS THE PASTOR ALWAYS RIGHT?

One of the most popular question in church leadership when there is a disagreement among members of the congregation "quote" the pastor is not always right. The truth of the matter none of the pastors and body of Christ is always right. According to our Lord and Saviour Jesus Christ none of us is right...He that is without sin among you, let him first the cast stone (John 8:7).

As it is written, There is none righteous, no, not one (Rom. 3:10). The issue here is not rather a pastor is always right but is he always "Righteous" let's established protocol with this question "Who Does The Church Belong To?" According to the Jews and and all Jesus nay-sayers opinions Jesus was never always right.

Let's call the roll of some of biblical characters wasn't always right who God call in leadership and he knew before he call them they wasn't right or righteous.

Old Testament: God knew before he created Adam he was going to sin in the garden of Eden God is foreknowledge. God knew Abraham was going to lie about Sarah being his wife and committed adultery with Hagar (Gen. 16:1-6) God called Moses to leadership to lead Israel out of Egypt when he saw Moses slew the Egyptian and hid him in the sand (Ex. 2:12) Was Moses right for killing the Egyptian?

Noah got drunk and he drank of the wine, and was drunken and he was uncovered in the tent (Gen. 9:21).

And David said unto Nathan, I have sinned against the Lord...2 Sam. 12:13

God already knew that all pastors before he assinged (hold responsible, appoint, ordain, commission) to all pulpits all over the world was already wrong like everybody else in the church. For all have sinned, and come short of the glory of God. (Rom. 3:23). God has never ordain a deacon to try to transform a pastor and God never ordain a Pastor to transform the pew.

Therefore if any man be in Christ, he is a new creature...2 Cor. 5:17 I believe we done forgot who the church belong to this raised the question why some churches can't keep pastors long because of our own ideas, and theology of how we think the church is to operate without never try to resolve a issue in the church with biblical truth.

New Testament characters God knew they wasn't right when God called them into the ministry. Peter denied Him (Matt. 26:70) Thomas doubted Him (Jn. 20:26-30) Judas Iscariot betrayed Him (Matt. 27:3).

Peter smote the high priest's servant, and cut off his right ear. The servant name was Malchus (John 18:10) Peter wrote 1 & 2 Peter.

Another popular term deacon use that is not in the bible the pastor supposed only take care of the spiritual things in the church and deacon take care the money or finances. The apostles handle the finances before the deacons. Having land, sold it, and brought the money, and laid it at the "Apostles" feet Acts 4:37; 35). According to Acts 20:28 Take heed unto yourselves, and to all the flock, over which the Holy Ghost hath made you ovreseers, to feed the church of God, which he hath purchased with his own blood. The pastor has every right to have a imput in everything goes on in the church because it is the Lord's Church the pastor must pastor the congregation as well as the money.

The traditon deacons think the only thing they supposed to do in the church is to count money and some of them is not paying their tithes and offering.

Another term not use in scripture that the pastor is the CEO Chief Executive Officer of the church.

According to the scriptures the pastor is the only position is a paid position in the church... for a workman is worthy of his hire (Matt. 10:10) many has taking this passage of scripture out of context Jesus was teaching and training a group of potential pastors and not a group of musicians, grass man, janitor, secretary. Many churches have experience some financial difficulty and the first salary they cut is the pastor.

According to Old Testament passages all the tithes and offering went to the priest and his family (Nu. 18:9-19)

New Testament passages Paul make mention about pastor being compensated then Jesus did.

For it written in the law of Moses, Thou shall not muzzle the ox that treadeth out the corn. Doth God take care for oxen (1 Cor. 9:9).

If we have sown unto you spiritual things, is it a great thing if we shall reap your carnal (money) things (1 Cor. 9:11).

Let the elders that rule well be counted worthy of double honour, especially they who labour in the word of God and doctrine (1 Tim. 5:17).

Elijah and the Widow Woman (1 Ki. 17:1-16).

The Pastor and the church feel like they are obligated to celebrate all positions because we have use a term that is not in the scriptures "if you do for one you got to do for the other" not according to scriptures.

If ye abide in me, and my words abide in you, ye shall ask what ye will, and it shall be done unto you (John 15:7)

There is no biblical truth that support these position who always tax the church with raises no money in the budget to reach the lost and backsliders or sinners. Any one who get paid in the church should tithe out their salary alone with other income they received from their jobs or government (Mal. 3:8-10; Lk. 6:38).

There are some things the pastor accept to keep harmony in the church to keep a position as pastor (Compromised).

Some paid positions in the church is sometimes is done with wrong motives (Money) both pastors and musicians.

According to scriptures all churches is to take total care of the Pastor and his Family. But we will give ourselves continually to prayer, and to the ministry of the word (Acts 6:4). If the devil can keep pastor off his knees busy with other things he overcommit himself to that's exactly what he the devil want he do not want a praying pastor or church

The thief cometh not, but to steal, and to kill, and to destroy: I am come that they might have life, and that they might have it more abundantly (John 10:10)

DEACONS LEADERSHIP PRAYER

Heavenly Father thank you for making me a saved born-again deacon who desire so much to a be New Testament deacon like the men of the model church in (Acts 6:1-7) and to be a faithful and loyal servant of the most high God, family man as well as to community. Our father thank you for every opportunity to attend Sunday School, Bible Study, and pay my tithes and offering (Heb. 10:25; Mal. 3:8-10). Our Father I pray I will always relieve my pastor of the responsibilites the divine Holy Spirit didn't assigned him.

Father I pray I will study the leadership style of Moses (Nu. 11:1-35; Ex. 18:1-27). Father I pray I will study the leadership style of our Lord and Saviour Jesus Christ (Matt. 1-28; Mk. 1-16; Lk. 1-24; Jn. 1-21).

Father I acknowledge the Holy Spirit the ultimate trainer of my Christian life by spending quality time with him in daily prayer and supplication (Phil. 4:6). O Lord help me to always remember my duties and assignments by the pastor and church make sure the water is ready for baptism, grass is cut, church clean, communion served, repair all maintenace problems, process the finances (Haggai 1:1-15; Psa. 24:1; 1 Cor. 14:33, 40).

Father I will obey my pastor: Obey them that have the rule over you, and submit yourselves: for they watch for your souls, as they must give account, that they may do it with joy, and not with grief: for that is unprofitable for you (Heb. 13:17). Father help me to remember to communicate with my pastor and leadership team about my absence from church, prayer meetings, team meetings, revivals, workshops, seminars all functions of the church (Heb. 13:16). Dear Lord I will not let the devil use me to fight and argue with the pastor during his tenure as pastor. Father help me to study the leadership style of the Acts of the Apostles that I may be an effective and fruitful deacon in the kingdom of God (Acts 1-28; Matt. 6:33).

Dear Lord help me fight the good fight of faith rather than fighting my pastor (1 Tim. 6:12). Father I pray you will bless me with wisdom and knowledge (Jas. 1:5; 2 Pt. 3:18) to control my tongue and to be a husband to my wife ruling our children in our home (1 Tim. 3:8, 12).

Dear Lord after I have been proved: (tested, trained) then let me use the office of a deacon, being found blameless (innocent) and help my wife not be a slanderer, but alert and faithful in all things as well as have a good degree of aptitude and attitude toward the things of God (1 Tim. 3:10, 11, 12, 13) and holding the mystery of the faith in a pure conscience (Matt. 5:8,1 Tim. 3:9, Heb. 11:6). mystery mean something difficult to know, unexplainable, unanswerable, irregularity, difficulty (Deut. 29:29).

THE STRUCTURE OF GOD'S ASSIGNMENT

Many in the body of Christ chose and select pastors according to personality, politics, favoritism (partiality). God make the assigment according to his SPIRITUALITY/ PERSONALITY. Jer. 3:15. The people of God are not trained to hear the voice of God. The church must recognize God, also assigns members to a local congregation to be shepherd by a assigned pastor. There are many makes commitment to the church and never make a commitment to the Lord Jesus Christ they get baptized and never come to Sunday School, Bible Study, pay tithes and offerings or sometimes never come back after baptism." For by one Spirit are we all baptized into one body...1 Cor. 12:13". The stucture of the body of Christ/Church does not aligned up with scriptures, there is no biblical doctrine as a organized church that has a "Co-Pastor" in the body of Christ. The scripture teaches us, For we are labourers together with God: ye are God's husbandry, ye are God's building. 1 Cor. 3:9. For ye are yet carnal: whereas there is among you envying, strife, divisions, are ye not carnal, and walk as men? 1 Cor. 3:3.

God's Purposed Who He Choses to Minister

The idea of preaching, is a tradition mindset, to think all preaching is to be in the pulpit, this is the reason the pulpit is filled with women who claim to be preachers. There are some pastors is very sensitive to this issue because they have put their wife or wives where God has not place them in their ministry. The bible does not support women preachers, the bible give references to women "ministers" God does not make mistakes, the bible mention in Matt. 8:14-17. And when Jesus was come into Peter's house, he saw his wife mother laid, sick and of a fever. And he touched her hand, and the fever left her: and she arose, and "ministered" unto them. And many women were beholding afar. off, which followed Jesus from Galilee, "ministering" unto him. Matt. 27:55. But we wil give ourselves continually to prayer, and to the "ministry" of the word Acts 6:4. The word "Minister" mean "Servant" we all are God's Servants. The word "Ministry" mean "Service" God has called all us to served Him, not all from the pulpit. Watchman Nee, in his book, The release of the Spirit, says ministering the Word mean Ministering the "Word" as a burden in our spirit.

The Holy Spirit does not inspire any female to apply for a vacant church/pulpit as a pastor, because it is not the divine of order of God. The husbands is not biblically sound in doctrine and trained by the Holy Spirit to teach his wife the divine order of God, both the layman, preachers, pastors, bishops, elders, etc. therefore the pulpit is used for any and everything. As I said earlier, the pulpit is THE AUTHORITY FIGURE OF CHRIST, where the PASTOR-TEACHER FEEDS THE SHEEPS/PEOPLES. Let's look at the three SPIRITUAL masculinity and nature of the Godhead. God the Father, God the Son, and God the Holy Spirit.

The word of God "Jesus Christ" In the beginning was the "WORD"...John 1:1 which is the AUTHORITATIVE—APPROVED, OFFICIAL. How can a all wise, intelligence God substitute his divine order of a Christ-figure (male) to a female figure (feminine) figure. There has been some wrong interpretation of the passage in Gal. 3:28 There is neither Jew nor Greek, there is neither bond nor free, there is neither male nor female: for ye are all one in Christ Jesus. This passage is dealing with "salvation" Paul, was addressing the Galatians concerning the law of uncircumcision, and women could not be circumcised. There is no such doctrine ordaining a female Bishop, the scriptures instructs us in 1 Tim. 3:2. A bishop then must be blameless (innocent) the "husband" of one wife...a female bishop does meet biblical quailfications from God perspective(viewpoint).

Paul, warned the Galatians church. I marvel that ye are so soon removed from him that called you into the grace of Christ unto another gospel. Which is not another; but there be some that trouble you, and would pervert (corrupt) the gospel of Christ. But though we, or an angel from heaven, preach any other gospel unto you than that which we have preached unto you, let him be accursed. As we said before, so say I now again, If any man preach any other gospel unto you than that ye have received, let him be accursed. For do I now persuade, or God? or do, I seek to please men? for if I pleased men., I should not be the servant of Christ. Gal. 1:6-10 Paul, urge the church of Corinth 1:10...and let there be no divisions among you.

God's Assigned Purposed for the Kingdom

There are many in the body of Christ who have not spent quality time with the Intelligence, all wise, God of the university, to know their purpose in the body of Christ. We have many acknowledging they been called to preach, then called to "salvation." The process of calling a pastor, sometimes the pulpit comittee don't know what their spiritual gifts is. The last two churches I pastored neither could answered my questions. 1. How do you know you're saved? 2. How do you introduced a person to Jesus Christ? 3. What is the gospel? 4. Who is Jesus and why should we believe in him. 5. What is the Church? These and many belivers of the body of Christ included leaders/pulpit/pew don't know the answer, yet trying to elect a pastor. 2 Tim. 2:15. There is a possibililties the lost trying to elect a lost pastor, it is very important the whole entire church pray SCRIPTURAL PRAYERS IN UNITY DAILY, AND WEEKLY, to know and train themselves in the word of God. There are some pastors use the church for a stepping stone and then they are gone. But he that is an hireling, and not the shepherd, whose own the sheep are not, seeth the wolf coming, and leaveth the sheep, fleeth: and the wolf catcheth them, and scattered the sheep. John 10:12

The process of calling a pastor ought to be the highest calling or election on the earth. Brethren, I count not my self to have apprehended: but this one thing I do, forgetting those things which are behind, and reaching forth unto those things which are before. I press toward the mark of the "high calling" of God in Christ Jesus. Phil. 3:13-14 This process ought to be a higher calling than the president of the United States of America, Because of the souls of mankind. Man's Eternal Security is at stake.

We spend more time in the body of Christ debating, dialoguing, arguing, divisions, on issues about women preaching, speaking in tongues, doctrine of denominations, whose going to hell or heaven, etc. I have not found in this region, State Convention, National Congress of Christian Education, churches, that has a strong, healthy, Evangelism and Prayer Ministry Team. The pupit is not making "Kingdom minded Disciples of Jesus Christ" every, preacher/pastor/churches, all to themselves, and by themselves. Black churches don't support and fellowship with one another. White churches afraid to fellowship in black neighborhood. Sunday is the most desegregated day of the week, how can we bridge the gap of Racism with this mentality. Reflecting passages: Endeavouring to keep the unity of the Spirit in the bond of peace. There is one body, and one Spirit, even as ye are called in one hope of your calling; One Lord, one faith, one baptism, One God and Father of all, who is above all, and through all, and in you all. Eph. 4:3-6.

Our cultural status is what's keeping the body of Christ divided and deliquent with effective prayer and evangelism ministry, the only time churches come together when there is National Disaster hit our country, town, city, state, community, funerals. The pulpit and pew only meet when they have to, not when they want to, it is difficult to get believers to support prayer meeting and bible study." But seek ye first the kingdom of God, and his righteousness; and all these things shall be added unto you. Matt. 6:33". The church want a pastor, but won't come to support Christian education training/learning. Not forsaking the assembling of ourselves together, as the manner of some is; but exhorting one one another: and so much the more, as ye see the day approaching. Heb. 10:25

Process   Progress   Success   Regress

1. The process, of calling a pastor to a vacant church, the church is considered vacant without a pastor, because without a pastor/undersheperd/shepherd/overseer, the church which is the body of baptized believers/sheeps, cannot live spiritually without proper shepherding, and nourishing of the word of God. Process, simply mean to make ready, or prepare for the journey of calling a pastor with knowledge, trust, and action by faith in God. Heb. 11:6. The process must begain with the pew allowing the Holy Spirit to bring about a transformation in the hearts, and minds, of the strongholds, prior to the newly elected pastor/leader arrived. The pulpit committee must Trust God's process by relying on the knowledge of scriptures to make a sound judgment of the candidate or the applicant. The Holy Spirit does not work, without the word. ...Without me you can do nothing. John 15:5. It is through the process God's way, that he fulfilled his promises. It is only through Christ we can experience his purpose, promise, and process, and spiritulaity.

2. To progress, simply mean to move forward, to advanced, the pulpit committee and the church must visit the church covenant on a regular basis in to have a healthy church and to have good church structure. Striving for Church Advancement, is to engage in the knowledge, of the work of the Holy Spirit, who make known Christ through our deeds and service. The church covenant, My sacred vows. written by: Albert Garner. Garner, ask some good questions, Let each ask himself, Do I strive hard to advance my church in knowledge? Do I strive to advance myself in knowledge of the Word of the Lord? The

term "strive" means to work hard, to labor strenuosly and earnestly. Church members should seek, strive, or work hard to increase in knowledge of the Lord, 2 Peter 3:18. God is more concerned about "SPIRITUAL GROWTH" in "HIS" Church. Churches doen't die, congregations die, the church is a spiritual organism, born again baptized believers of Jesus Christ with the indwelling of the Holy Spirit. Congregation is a group of unsaved, unregenerated, unconverted that gather together at church, work, wherever. The church is much smaller than congregation.

3. Success, is also progress, to achieve, to accomplished as well as advanced. Many Pastors and Churches measure success by how many members, and, edifices they have, success from God's perspective is found in "Matt. 18:20 For where two or three are gathered together in my name, there am I in the midst of them". Success, God's way is what he told Joshua. "Only be thou strong and courageous, that thou mayest observe to do according to all the law, which Moses my servant commanded thee: turn not from it to the right hand or to the left, that thou mayest prosper whithersoever thou goest. This book of the law shall not depart out of thy mouth; but thou shall meditate therein day and night, that thou mayest observe to do according to all that is written therein: for then thou shalt make thy way prosperous, and then thou shalt have good (success). Have not I have commanded thee? Be strong and of a good courage: for the Lord thy God is with thee whithersoever thou goest. Joshua 1:7-9." Every successor should acknowledge those who have gone on ahead them, no matter what the circumstances and speak well of them to the congregations. This will "glorify" God in heaven. God assigns pastors to churches and God assings churches to pastors he don't give churches to pastors, there is only two peoples think the church belong to them, the pastors, and the members. ... and upon this rock I will build "my" church. Matt. 18:18

4. Regress, simply mean to go backward, without good spiritual sound biblical discernment of the Holy Spirit a untrained pupit and untrained pew can destroy the predecessor success. All that our forefathers work hard for, can crumbled without good strong leadership ministry. There will also be a regress without proper leadership skills and development, you can have a P.H.D. and a master of divinity, and still regress. P.H.D can mean, "Post Hole Digger" without proper training. The problem is the pulpit and the pew trying to master God/divinity. The body of Christ does not spend time with the Holy Spirit for him to train us how to listen to him. Pastors, too, insecure, and jealous, bitter, anger, envy, pride, and inconsiderate of one another, they don't seek other resources to help

their (God's) peoples. This generation of young pastors have no visions, goals, strategies, for church growth and development, no shepherd's heart for souls, they only have a microphone ministry. "Where there is no visions, the people perish...Pr. 29:18." "My people are destroyed for lack of knowledge...Hos. 4:6. There's always going to be church vacancies. Pastors are looking some stepping stones churches, not to Shepherd, but as a partime job. When the church start regressing they run and find them another church to regress it.

Jesus Trained The Twelve

CHURCH STRUCTURE

PASTOR/DEACONS BIBLICAL RELATIONSHIP

WORK ETHICS

BIBLICAL EXAMPLES:

1. Pastor must acknowledge he needs help to do ministry and seek God through prayer for the persons to fit the team. And it came to pass in those days, that he went out into a mountain to pray, and continue all night in prayer to God. And when it was day, he called unto him his disciples: and of them he chose twelve, whom also he named apostles. Lk. 6:12-13

2. And they appointed two, Joseph called Barsabas, who was surnamed Justus, and Matthias. And they prayed, and said, Thou, Lord, which knowest the hearts of all men, shew whether of these two thou hast chosen. That he may take part of this ministry and apostleship, from which Judas by transgression fell, that he might go to his own place. And they gave forth their lots; (votes) and the lot (vote) fell upon Matthias; and he was numbered with the eleven apostles. Note: no, Dvd, resume,' The eleven apostles was the quote unquote the pulpit committee they totally relied on the Holy Spirit in "PRAYER." Acts 1:22-26

TEAMWORK CONCEPT:

1. I am not able to bear this people alone, because it is too heavy for me. and if thou deal thus with me, kill me, I pray thee, out of hand, if I have found favor in thy sight; and let me not see my wretchedness. (destruction, wear away, burnouts) Numbers 11:14-15

2. And the Lord said unto Moses, Gather unto me seventy men of the elders of Israel, whom thou knowest to be the elders of the people, and officers over them; and bring them unto the tabernacle of the congregation, "that they may stand there with thee." Numbers 11:16

3. And it came to pass on the morrow, that Moses sat to judge the people: and the people stood by Moses from morning unto the evening. And Moses' father in law saw all that he did to the people, he said, what is this thing that thou doest to the people? why sittest thou thyself "alone" and all the people stand by thee from morning unto even? And Moses said unto his father in law, Because the people come unto me to enquire of God: And when they have a matter, they come unto me; and I judge between one another; and I do make the m know the statutes of God, and his laws.

And Moses' father in law said unto him, The thing that thou doest is not good. Thou wilt surely "wear away," both thou and the people that is with thee: for this thing is "too heavy" (too much) for thee: "thou art not able to perform it thyself alone." Hearken now unto my voice, I will give thee counsel, and God shall be with thee: Be thou for the people to God-ward, that thou mayest bring the causes unto God." And thou "shalt teach" them ordinances and laws, and shalt shew them the way wherein they must walk, and the work that they must do.

Moreover thou shalt provide out of all the people "able (committed, devoted, dedicated) men, such as fear God, men of truth, hating covetousness: and place such over them, to be rulers of thousands, and rulers of hundreds, rulers of fifties, and rulers of tens. (rulers/spiritual leaders/teamwork. And let (permit, authorized)them judge the people all the seasons: (times) and it shall be, that every great matter they shall bring unto thee, "Pastor" but every small matter they (deacons) shall judge: so shall it be easier for thyself, and they (deacons) shall bear the burden with thee.

If thou shalt do this thing, and God command thee so, then thou shalt be able to endure, and all this people (church/congregation shall also go to their place in peace. (with joy) So Moses hearkened (listened) to the voice of his father in law, and did all that he had said. (wisdom) And Moses chose able men (committed, devoted, dedicated) out of all Israel, (church) and made them heads (spiritual leaders/team leaders/overseers/deptartment heads over the people, (not Moses/Pastor). rulers of thousands, rulers of hundreds, rulers of fifties, and rulers of tens. (families, members of the congregations). And they (deacons) judge the people at all the seasons: (times) the hard causes (diffulty,prayerful, situations, circumstances) they brought unto Moses, but every small matter they(deacons) judge themselves. And Moses let his father in law depart; (go) and he went his way into his own land. Ex. 18:13-27

THE LEADERSHIP STYLE OF JESUS
THE JESUS "TEAM" CONCEPT

1. And when he had called unto him his twelve disciples, he gave them power against unclean spirits, to cast them out, and to heal all manner of sickness and all manner of disease. And the names of the twelve apostles are these: The first, Simon, who called Peter, and Andrew his brother; James the son of Zebedee, and John his brother; Philip, and Bartholomew; Thomas, and Matthew the publican; James the son of Alphaeus, and Lebbaeus, whose surname was Thaddaeus; Simon the canaanite, and Judas Iscariot, who also btrayed Christ. These twelve Jesus sent forth, and commanded them, saying, Go..... Matt. 10:1-5

Jesus Ordains Twelve Disciples

And he ordained twelve, "that they should be with him," and that he might send them forth to preach. And to have power to heal sickness, and to cast to out devils. (The same twelve) Simon he surname Peter; And James the son of Zebedee, and John the brother of James; and he surnamed them Boanerges, which is, The sons of thunder; And Andrew, and Philip, and Bartholomew, and Matthew, and Thomas, and James the son Alphaeus, and Thaddaeus, and Simon the cannanite, And Judas Iscariot, which also betrayed him: and they went into an house. Mark 3:13-19

Seventy Sent Forth

After these things the Lord appointed other seventy also, and sent them two and two before his face into every city and place, whither he himself would come. Therefore said he unto them, The harvest truly is great, but the labourers are few: pray ye therefore the Lord of the harvest, that he would send forth labourers into "HIS' harvest. Go your ways.... LK. 10:1-3

The Twelve Apostles/Church/Deacons/Team Concepts

And in those days, when the number of the disciples was multiplied, there arose a murmuring of the Grecians against the Hebrews, because their widows were neglected in the daily ministration. Then the twelve called the multitude of the disciples unto them, and said, It is not reason that we should leave the word of God, and served tables. Wherefore, brethren, look ye out among seven men of honest report, full of the Holy Ghost and wisdom, whom we may appoint over this business. But we will give ourselves continually to "prayer," and to the ministry of the "word." And the saying pleased the whole multitude: "church" and they chose Stephen, a and man full of "faith" and of the Holy Ghost, and Philip, and Prochorus, and Nicanor, and Timon, Parmeans, and Nicolas a proselyte of Antioch. Whom they set before the apostles: and when they had prayed, they laid their hands on them. And the word of God increased; and the number of the disciples multiplied in Jerusalem "greatly;" and a great company of the priest were "obedient to the faith."

The seven men were the "idea of a biblical deacon" verses a tradition deacons they did not fight or argue with their Spiritual leader. And the multitude of them that believed were of one heart and one soul: neither said any of them that ought of the things which he possessed was his own; but they had all things common. Acts 4:32 The model church did not argue over finances or money, Neither was there any among them that lacked: for as many were possessors of lands or houses sold them, and brought the prices of things that was sold. And laid them down at the apostles' feet: And hath put all things under his feet... Eph. 1:22 and distribution was made unto every man according as he had need. Having land, sold it, and brought the money, and laid at the apostles' feet. Acts 4:34, 35, 37. There is nothing wrong with pastors or deacons counting money but it is wrong to think they are the only ones that can count it. We need not put too much emphasis on titles to get the job done.

God the Father, God the Son, God the Holy Spirit/Team Concepts

Go ye therefore, and teach all nations, baptizing them in the name of the Father, and of the Son, and of the Holy Ghost: Matt. 28:19

There were four gospel writers/Team Concept

Matthew   Mark   Luke   John

Five Gifts To the Body of Christ/Team Concept

And he gave some, apostles; and some prophets; and some evangelist; and some pastors and teachers. Eph. 4:11

Moses and Joshua/Team Concept

And Joshua the son of nun was full of the spirit of wisdom; For Moses had laid his hands upon him: and the children of Israel hearkened unto him, and as the Lord commanded Moses. Deut. 34:9

Paul and Timothy/Team Concept

To Timothy, my dearly beloved son: Grace mercy and peace, from God the Father and Christ Jesus our Lord. 2 Timothy 1:2

Paul and Silas/Team Concepts

Then he called for a light, and sprang in, and came trembling, and fell down before Paul and Silas. Acts 16:29

Pastor and Deacon/Team Concept

And I will give you pastors according to my heart, which shall feed you with knowledge and understanding. Jer. 3:15 And let these also be proved: then let them use the office of a deacon, being found blameless (innocent, not guilty).

Husband and Wife /Team Concept

...but as for me and my house, we will serve the Lord. Joshua 24:15

Choir/Praise team/Concept

Sing unto the Lord, bless his name; shew forth his salvation from day to day. Psalm 96:2 Sing unto the Lord a new song; for he hath done marvellous things: his right hand, and his holy arm, hath gotten him the victory. Psalm 98:1

Usher/Team Concept

For a day in thy courts is better than a thousand. I had rather be a doorkeeper in the house of my God, than to dwell in the tents of the wicked. Psalm 84:10

Trustee/Team Concept

Trust in the Lord with all thine heart; and lean not unto thine own understanding. Pr. 3:5

Mother Board/Team Concept

When I call to remembrance the unfeigned faith that is in thee, which dwelt first In thy grandmother Lois, and thy mother Eunice; and I am persuaded that is in thee also. 2 Ti. 1:5

Youth/Team Concept

Remember thy Creator in the days of thy youth. Eccl. 12:1. Flee also youthful lusts. 2 Ti. 2:22

Children/Team Concept

And thou shalt teach them diligently unto thy children. Children, obey your parents in the Lord. Deut. 6:7 Ehp. 6:1

Janitor/Team Concept

Is it time for you, O ye, to dwell in your ceiled houses, and this house lie waste? Haggai 1:4

Kitchen Committee/Team Concept

...Whence shall we buy bread, that these may eat. John 6:5

Sunday School/Team Concept

Not forsaking the assembling of ourselves together as the manner some is. Heb. 10:25

Bible Study/Team Concept

Study to shew thyself approved unto God. 2 Ti. 2:15

Teachers/team Concept

Or ministry, let us wait on our ministering: or he that teacheth, on teaching. Ro. 12:7

Lawn/Team Concept

The grass withereth, the flower fadeth: but the word of our God shall stand forever. Isa. 40:8

Men/Team Concept

And he spake a parable unto them to this end, that men ought always to pray, and not to faint. LK. 18:1

Women/Team Concept

Therefore many of them believed; also honourable women which were Greeks, and of men, not a few. Acts 17:12

Saint and Sinner/Team Concept

Then drew near unto him all the pulicans and sinners for to hear him. And the Pharisees and scribes murmured, saying, This man receiveth sinners, and eateth with them. Lk. 15:1-2

The Church/Team Concept

Behold, how good and how pleasant it is for brethren to dwell together in unity. Psalm 133:1 Endeavouring to keep the unity of the Spirit in the bond of peace. Eph. 4:3

There is no "I" in Team.

Take the "I" out of pride before it take you for a ride. quote: Michael Day

Three/Team Concept

For there are three that bear record in heaven, the Father, the Word, and the Holy Ghost: and these three are one. 1 John 5:7

Three /Team Concept

And there are three that bear witness in earth, the Spirit, and the water, and the blood: and these three are one. 1 John 5:8

Three/Team Concept

And after six days Jesus taketh Peter, James, and John...Matt. 17:1

Three/Team Concept

And he commanded the most mighty men that were in his army to bind Shadrach, Meshach, and Abednego, and to cast them into the burning fiery furnace. Dan. 3:20

Two or Three/Team Concept

For where two or three are gathered together in my name am I in the midst of them. Matt. 18:20

Ten/Team Concept

And as he entered into a certain village, there met him ten that were lepers, which stood afar off: Lk. 17:12

Crucifixion/Burial/Resurrection/Team Concept

And that he was buried, and that he rose again the third day according to the scriptures. 1 Cor. 15:4

Twelve Tribes of Israel/Team Concept

Now these are the names of the children of Israel, which came into Egypt; every man and his household came with Jacob. Reuben, Simeon, Levi, and Judah, Issachar, Zebulun, and Benjamin, Dan, and Naphtali, Gad, and Asher. Ex. 1:1-4 ....for Joseph was in Egypt in already Ex. 1:5

PASTOR'S COMPENSATION/STRAGETY

The pastor and the congregation must have good working relationship with one another to compensate and or negotiate a good benefit package.

Negotiate-make peace, contract, make the best, agreement, discussion. The church and pastor can agree on the following: "Breathing Room" (Options)

1. Pastor keep a low paid salary.
2. Church pays half or all house note.
3. Church pay half or all cell phone bill.
4. Church pay half or all utility bill.
5. Church make "Budget" for Pastor and his Family.
6. Church help with half or all medical expenses.
7. Church celebrate "Pastor's National Day

The Church Cannot do enough for God's Anointed One, God's Chosen Vessel, God's Servants, The Man of God, The Angel of God's Bride, God' Shepherd/Under Shepherd.

For God is not unrighteous to forget your work and labour of love, which ye shewed toward his name, in that ye have ministered to the saints, and do minister (Heb. 6:10)

And to esteem them very highly in love for their work's sake. And at peace among yourselves (1 Thess. 5:13)

These strageties can help the pastors devote himself with spending "Quality Time" WITH THE MASTER (Acts 6:4).

8. Church celebrate Pastor's Appreciation Day

Appreciate mean (to be grateful, welcome, pay respects to, be indebted, feel or be obligated, acknowledge, never forget, overflow with gratitude, to reconize worth, esteem, honor, praise, admire, like.

Appreciation mean (sense of gratitude, thankfulness, recognition, gratefulness, (Favorable Opinion) esteem, high regard, enjoyment, appreciativeness, love, affection senitivity,

Appreciative mean thankful, appreciatory, indebted, cooperative, aware, favorable, satisfied, considerate, friendly kindly, gladdened. Ant. opposite: unfriendly, cold, hostile.

9. Church pay half or all vacation.
10. Church pay all expenses of Christian Edcation: College, Leadership Training (Seminars, Workshops, etc.)
11. Church pay half or all Wardrode cleaning (Suits, shirts, etc.)
12. Church have "Book Budget" to purchase books to study.
13. Church pay half or all car note.

GETHSEMANE/AGONY/OIL PRESS

MATT. 26:36-46; MK. 14:32-42; LK. 22:39-46;

JHN. 18:1-2

AGONY IN THE PULPIT

AGONY IN THE PEW

Gethsemane—hebrew mean gat shmanim (oil press) a urban garden at the foot of the Mount of Olives in Jerusalem, a important place where Jesus prayed and his disciples were sleep while He prayed.

Jesus sweat as great drop of blood falling to the ground (Lk. 22:44). Indian Journal Dermatology. A word called Hematohidrosis—A Rare Clinical Phenomenon a very rare condition in which human being sweats blood.

Hematohidrosis also known as Hematidrosis, hemidrosis and hematidrosis, is a condition in which capillary blood vessels that feed the sweat glands rupture, causing them to exude (discharge, sweat) ocurring underconditions of extreme physical or emotional stress.

Manonulkul et al. proposed the term "hematofolliculohidrosis" because it appeared along with sweat-like fluid and blood exuded via the follicular canal—one-celled. Another type of of bleeding through skin is psychogenic stigmata; a term used to signify areas of scars, open wounds or bleeding through the unbroken skin.

Patients belonging to this group were found to be frequently neurotic. The clinical finding of this type are a slight elevation of the skin before prolonged oozing of blood, a peasized bluish discoloration on patient's palm and ersipelas-like leison. This type of bleeding whenever is from old scars of serious anxiety.

AGONIZE—Struggle, suffer.

AGONIZING—Struggling, tormenting, disturbing, painful.

AGONY—Suffering, torture, anguish, pain.

Agony in the pulpit is caused by a untrained pulpit and untrained pew. The ultimate teacher and guide for the pulpit is the Holy Spirit. The pastor has to deal with non-biblical deacons and church members. And the deacons and members has to deal with non-biblical trained pastors. Sometimes the pulpiteers has aready has had seminary training and fail to teach traditions out of people and the newly elected pastor go to a church knocking down walls of traditions and knock himself out of a church.

Gethsemane mean oil press pastors anoint members with oil and the pastors stay under pressure more than the members do. The greatest struggle a pastor has is to make him some good quality leaders that will commit to his leadership ability. It is very painful to the pastor when he has a board of unfaithful, unsaved, unconverted, unconcerned, undedicated, unproductive, uncommitted deacon board who has no prior leadership training prior to becoming a deacon. "Moreover it is required in stewards, that a man be found faithful" (1 Cor. 4:2). Lay hands suddenly on no man...(1 Tim. 5:22).

My personal commentary if the pastor has to do all the work in the church what do he needs with deacons. Pastors must be trained to trained his followers most of the pastors and members burnouts is caused by overcommitment with duties and responsibilities.

A pastor friend of mine shared with me he was cutting the church grass and the deacon driving down the street blowing his horn at him while he cutting grass.

Another pastor friend of mine shared with me he was tired and burnout as pastor because members leave him in the church fellowship hall cleaning up after annual day meal.

Another pastor experience the pain and suffering from deacons excuses fo not preparing the water for baptism and he had to go to the church to prepare for baptism.

Deacons like the title rather than the commitment, services, responsibilities, and being a devoted servant of Jesus Christ. Many in the body of Christ is more title minded rather than Christ minded, mission minded, and kingdom minded. Deacons are more money minded and more misery minded when they can't have their way with the pastor. Tradition deacon want to control the pastor.

The seven men in Acts 6:1-7 that was selected by the multitudes were business minded men honest report if a deacon does not give God the tithes and offering he is not making an honest report the church rather he work or on fixed income. If deacons does not attend Sunday School and Bible Study how can he be a help or blessing to the pastor and the church.

I personally believed these seven men was a member of the model church. "Then they that gladly received his word were baptized: and the same day there were added unto them about three thousand souls. And they "continue stedfastly in the apostles' doctrine" and fellowship, and in breaking of bread, and in prayers. And fear came upon every soul: and many wonders and signs were done by the apostles. And all that "believed" were together, and had all things common. And sold their possessions and goods, and parted them to all men, as every man had need. And they, "continuing" daily with one accord in the temple, breaking bread from house to houise, did eat their meat with gladness and singleness (motive) of heart. Praising God, and having favour with all the people. And the Lord added to the church daily such as should be saved. Acts 2:41-47.

Pastors often put themselves in these positions of overcommitment by poor leadership stucture. The agony and agonizing of leadership is pastors has no breathing room in ministry. Author and writer Sandra Stanley book "Breathing" Room" said, we often has to Cram some time in for God it's difficult to get members to attend prayer service and bible class.

I personally feel that every Sunday oft to be family time there is nothing in scriptures of the New Testament church we called the model (set an example) church. Tradition is what killing our churches and her purpose and mission (Matt. 28:18-20). The mission of the church is not to pay utility bills, bury those who doesn't have life insurance policy, saved money, the church has been called to lead souls to Christ to be saved.

The pew is experiencing agony because they're not adequately being nuture the Word of God the church has become a revolving door both for the pulpit and pew. The pulpit because poor struture some churches have not been properly train to care for a pastor full time and his tenure is short lived some pastors used a church for a stepping stone until he find a better benefit package at another church. Sometimes pastors make the mistake thinking he is getting a better position and lose a good church sometimes it's greed God never told him to go to another church.

What's more agonizing in the pulpit is pastors is not spending "Quality" time with God for God to give "Visions" to move the church forward. And when God give the "Visions" pastors don't have the faith to fulfilled the visions because sometimes pastors and deacons is more money minded than mission minded and fail to to do outreach mininstry or fulfilled the Great Commision (Matt. 28:18-20). The pain or the agony of the pulpit is not winning the lost it is people not paying their tithes and offering most pastors does not own or have a healthy library and have poor study habits you can tell by listen to the radio and television.

Some pastors are more frustrated over the pew not giving their tithes and offering than they are a soul not giving their life to Christ. There is no eternal security in tithes and offerings there is no eternal security in no pulpit there is no eternal security in women preachers there is no eternal security in speaking in tongues these and many other issues has got the body of Christ divided everything that sound good is not always sound doctrine.

Some pastors have very little faith to do ministry some pastors is totally relying on the church budget to take him and his family than they are on God. I personally think it is poor church structure for a pastor have money to do radio and T.V. ministry and have members to sell tickets to finance their love day. Pastors is not other churches pastor.

The agony of the pew is complaining about blessing their pastor on pastor and wife appreciation day. There are some bitterness among some of the members of the body of Christ concerning this matter.

Some members in the body of Christ is out growing their pastor's intellectual ability to minister and rightly divide the Word of God because some pastors does not seek after "QUALITY" LEADERSHIP TRAINING" for the congregations some churches invest their money in church community picnic and revivals and no investment in Evangelism Training To Make Disciples. The church cannot grow without biblical sound doctrine and a variety of ministries to accomodate worshipers. There is so much "Vandalism" because there is no "Evangelism."

If my people, which are called by my name, shall humble themselves, and pray, and seek my face, and turn from their wicked ways: then will I hear from heaven, and will forgive their sin, and will heal their land. 1 Chr. 7:14.

The harvest is past, the summer is ended, and we are not "saved." Jer. 8:20

And brought them out, and said, Sirs, what must I do to be "Saved?" Acts 16:30

That if thou shalt confess with thy mouth the Lord Jesus, and shalt believe in thine heart that God hath raised him from the dead. Rom. 10:9

CALLING A PASTOR TO A VACANT CHURCH GOD'S WAY

ISA. 55:8-9

PASTOR, NOW WHAT?

I have in my library a book by T.D. Jake, "So You Call Yourself a Man?" My question to a newly elected pastor and already existing pastor. So you call yourself a "Pastor?" Just a quick survey and examination: What are your visions for God's divine assingment where he has place you.

* What are your goals and church growth strageties to move the church forward?

* What curriculum do you have for the church Christian Education program?

* Were you active in Sunday School, Bible study, and pay your tithes and offerings, as an associate minister?

* Why do you want to be a Pastor any way? 1 Tim. 3:1

* What is the first thing you're going to change as the newly elected pastor? Mk. 7:5

* Now that you're a pastor do you have your wife under control? 1 Tim. 3:4

* As a pastor, are you in God's alignment for his assignment? Jer. 29:11

* Are you faithful to God? 1 Cor. 4:2

* Are you faithful to your family? Josh. 24:15

* Are you faithful to the church? Heb. 10:25

* Are you active or faithful in the community? Acts 2:41-47

* Are you faithtful and communicate with your pastor? Heb. 13:16-17

* What is your motive to be a pastor? Acst 8:20-22

* Are you willing to relocate at the church expense? Mal. 3:8-10

Now that you're a pastor:

What is a pastor? What is the responsibilities of a pastor? Why does the church need a pastor?

A pastor is an overseer/undershepherd/ that sheperds or feeds the Word of God to God's peoples. Jer. 3:15, John 10:11, John 21:15-17, 1 Pt. 5:2. The responsibilities of the pastor are to perform communion, baptism, weddings, funerals, counseling, as well as other worship services. Pastor and Teacher. Ehp. 4:11. The church needs a pastor because the scriptures say, How shall they call on him in whom they have not believed? and how shall they believe in him of whom they have not heard? and how they shall they hear without a preacher?

And how shall they preach, except they be sent? as it is written, How beautiful are the feet of them that preach the gospel of peace, and bring glad tidings of good things. Ro. 10:14-15. The "pastor" or the "man of God" served as the "Authority Figure" (Christ) of the Church. And the "WORD" of God served as the "Authoritative" of the "CHURCH."

Why Churches Go Through So Many Pastors?

Some Reasons/Tenures:

1. Infidelity
2. Lack of prayers
3. Pay
4. Untrained pulpit
5. Untrained pew
6. Poor structure
7. Poor leadership
8. Lack of fastings
9. Pay/benefits
10. No visions.

THE PROCESS OF CALLING A PASTOR TO A VACANT CHURCH

GOD'S WAY

ISAIAH 55:8-9

LISTENING   LEARNING   LEADING

To be an effective leader one must be willing to listen to the voice of the Holy Spirit. Again, he limited in a certain, saying in David, Today, after so long a time; as it is said, Today if ye will hear his voice, harden not your hearts. Heb. 4:7. To be an effective leader one must be willing to learn from others. But ye have not so learned Christ. Eph. 4:20. Take my yoke upon you, and learn of me; for I am meek and lowly in heart: and ye shall find rest unto your souls. As a leader one must be willing to lead. The Lord is my shepherd; I shall not want. He maketh me to lie down in green pastures: He leadeth me beside the still waters. He restoreth my soul: he leadeth me in the paths of righteousness for his name sake. Psa. 23:1-2

Only God Knows A Person Character

God's way is not our way of calling a person to a vacant church/pulpit by depending on the secular world by way of news paper,social media, or dvd, etc. The scripture says, The heart is deceitful above all things, and desperately wicked: WHO CAN KNOW IT? Jer. 17:9. O LORD, thou hast searched me, and known me. Thou knowest my down sitting and mine uprising, thou understandest my thought a far off. Thou compassest my lying down, and art acquainted with all my ways. There is not a word in my tongue, but, lo, O Lord, thou knowest it altogether. Thou hast beset me behind and before, and laid thine hand upon me. Search me, O God, and know my heart: try me, and know my thoughts. My substance was not hid from thee, when I was made in secret, and curiously wrought in the lowest parts of the earth. Thine eyes did see my substance, yet being unperfect; and in thy books all my members were written which in continue were fashioned, when as yet there was none them. Search me, O God, and know my heart: try me, and know my thoughts. Psa. 139:1-5,15,16,23

How We Can Know Who To Chose

It is only through SCRIPTURAL PRAYERS the church is safe and sure. O LORD, you said, The steps of a good man is ordered by the Lord: and he delighted in his way. Psa. 37:23 O LORD, you said, Trust in the Lord with all thine heart; and lean not unto thine own understanding. In all thine ways acknowledge him, and he shall direct thy paths. Pr. 3:5-6. O LORD, I know that the way of man is not in himself: it is not in man that waiketh to direct his steps. Jer. 10:23 ...for without me ye can do nothing. John 15:5. Totally depend on the chief Shepherd. And when the chief Shepherd shall appear, ye shall receive a crown of glory that fadeth not away. 1 peter 5:4. Totally depend on the good Shepherd. I am the good shepherd: the good shepherd giveth his life for the sheep. I am the good shepherd, and know my sheep, and known of mine. Therefore doth my Father love me, because I lay down my life, that I might take it again. No man taketh it from me, but I lay it down of myself. I have power to lay it down, and I have power to take it again. This commandment have I received of my Father. John 10:11, 14, 17, 18. The church must returned to the Shepherd who is the Bishop of our souls 1 Peter 2:25.

Carnal Minds Trying To Make A Divine Assignment

For we know that the law is carnal, sold under sin. Ro. 7:14. There is therefore now no condemnation to them which are in Christ Jesus who walk not after the flesh, but in the Spirit. For the law of Spirit of life in Christ Jesus hath made me free from the law of sin and death. For what the law could not do, in that it was weak through the flesh. God sending his own Son in the likeness of sinful flesh, and for sin, condemned sin in the flesh: That the righteousness of the law might be fulflilled in us, who walk not after the flesh, but after the Spirit. For to be carnally minded is death; but to be spiritually minded is life and peace. Because the carnal (WORLDLY) mind is enmity (animosity, malice, hatred) against God: for it is not subject to the law of God, neither indeed can be. So then they that are in the flesh cannot please God. But ye are not in the flesh, but in the Spirit, if so be that the Spirit of God dwell in you. Now if any man have not the Spirit of Christ, he is none of his. And if Christ be in you, the body is dead because of sin; but the Spirit is life because of righteousness. But if the Spirit of him raised up Jesus from the dead shall also quicken your mortal bodies by his Spirit that dwelleth in you. Ro. 8:1-11 notice: omitted v.5. For as many as are led by the Spirit of God, they are the sons of God. Ro. 8:14.

The Pulpit Committee and God/Quality Time

The pulpit committee must spend quality time in the presence of God persistently to be able to receive quality discernment and meditation and wisdom to make the recommendation to body of Christ for sound judgment of choice of which candidate. ... to another discerning of spirits 1 Cor. 12:10. For as the body is one, and hath many members and all the members of that one body, being many, are one body: so also is Christ. 1 Cor. 12:12. It is very important that personal and corporate prayers be done daily and weekly schedule for God to make his divine assingment sooner than later. If any of you lack wisdom, let him ask of God, that giveth to all men liberally, and upbraideth not; and it shall be given him. Jas. 1:5

The psalmist urge togetherness, Behold, how good and how pleasant it is for brethren to dwell together in unity. Psa. 133:1. As I said earlier there must be a on continuation of SCRIPTURAL PRAYERS. ...that men ought always to pray, and not to faint. (Quit). Lk. 18:1. And, behold, the angel of the Lord came upon him, and a light shined in the prison: and he smote Peter on the side, and raised him up, saying, Arise up quickly. And his chains fell off from his hands.

And the angel said unto him, Gird thyself, and bind on thy sandals. And so he did. And he saith unto him, Cast thy garment about thee, and follow me. And he went out, and followed him; and wist not that it was true which was done by the angel; but thought he saw a vision. When they were past the first and the second ward, they came unto the iron gate that leadeth unto the city; which opened to them of his own accord: and they went out, and passed on through one street; ; and forthwith the angel departed from him.

And when Peter was come to himself, he said, Now I know of asurety, that the lord hath sent his angel, and hath delivered me out of the hand of Herod, and from all the expectation of the people of the Jews. And when he had considered the thing, he came to the house of Mary the mother of John, whose surname was Mark; wher many gathered together "PRAYING." And as Peter knocked at the door of the gate, a damsel came to hearken, named Rhoda. And when she knew Peter's voice, she opened not the gate for gladness, but ran in, and told how Peter stood before the gate. And they said unto her, Thou art mad. But she constantly affirmed that it was even so. Then said they, it is his angel. Peter continued knocking: and when they had opened the door, and saw him, they were astonished, But he, beckoning unto them with the hand to hold their peace, declared unto them how the Lord had brought him out of the prison, And he said, Go shew these things unto James, and to the brethren. And he departed, and went into another place. Acts 12:7-17

The Pastors Hold The Keys To the Kingdom

When Jesus came into the coast of Caesarea Philippi, he asked his disciples, saying, Whom do men say that I the Son of man am? And they said, Some say that thou art John the Baptist: some, Elias; and others, Jeremias, or one of the prophets. He saith unto them, But whom say ye that I am? And Simon Peter answered and said, Thou art the Christ, the Son of the living God. And Jesus answered and said unto him, Blessed art thou, Simon Barjona: for flesh and blood hath not revealed it unto thee, but my Father which is in heaven. And I say also unto thee, That thou art Peter, and upon this rock I will build my church; and the gates of hell shall not prevail against it. And I will give unto thee the keys of the kingdom of heaven: and whatsoever thou shalt bind on earth shall be bound in heaven: and whatsoever thou shalt loose on earth shall be loose in heaven. Matt. 16:13-19

I srongly believed that the body of Christ is in great need of Christian Leadership Training to educate the pulpit and the pew. The doctrine of the baptist denomination believed the Holy Spirit makes the divine assignment many of the baptist faith has not had a good and healthy training of the doctrine of the Holy Spirit. I believed this is the reason why the baptist churches remain vacant such a long time. It seems as though the churches is not sensitive the voice of the Holy Spirit. Take heed therefore unto yourselves, and to all the flock, over the which the Holy Ghost hath made you overseers, to feed the church of God, which he hath purchased with his own blood. Acts 20:28

There Is A Lack Of Training/Teaching On Biblical Doctrine

Example:

* Salvation   *Holy Spirit   *Sin   * Church   *God   *Jesus   *Christ
     * Repentance

* Conversion   *Prayer   *Faith   *Trinity   *Grace   *Mercy   *Saved
     *Born again

*Redemption   *Regeneration   *Eternal Security   *Satan and Demons
     *Heaven

*Hell   *Sanctification   *Predestination   *Stewardship   *Communion

*Baptism   *Family   *Preaching   *Forgivingness   *How to call a pastor   *Praise

*Worship   *Evangelism   *The Gospel   *Christ Return   *Pastoring
     *Spiritual Gifts

* Preaching   *Body of Christ   *Laying on of Hands   *Apostles   *Benediction

*Holiness   *Crime and Racism   *Closing The Backdoor of the Church
     *Sunday School

*Bible Study   *Portraying the Model Church   *How to study the Bible
     *How can I be sure of my Salvation?

CALLING A PASTOR TO A VACANT CHURCH GOD'S WAY

Isaiah 55:8-9

"P" Team

1. ....Prayer Lk. 18:1

2. ....Person Eccl. 12:13

3. ....Preacher Eccl. 1:1

4. ....Pastor Jer. 3:15

5. ....Pulpit Neh. 8:4

6. ....Personality 2 Cor. 5:17

7. ....Power Acts 1:8

8. ....Paradise Lk. 23:43

9. ....Partaker Heb. 2:14

10. ....Purpose Ro. 8:28

11. ....Passion Jas. 5:17

12. .... Perform Phil. 1:6

13. .... Pardon Isa. 55:7

14. .... Peace John 16:33

15. .... Praise Psa. 150:6

Unity

LET US RIDE THIS TRAIN OF CHRISTIAN EDUCATION TOGETHER

AND

TRAIN THE BODY OF CHRIST TOGETHER

FROM A BIBLICAL PERSPECTIVE:

PREPARING THE BODY OF CHRIST

FOR

THE RETURN OF CHRIST

NETWORKING FOR THE KINGDOM OF GOD

Supporting scriptures:

Behold, how good and how pleasant it is for brethren to dwell together in unity. Ps. 133:1

And all that believed were together.....Acts 2:44

Endeavouring to keep the unity of the Spirit in the bond of peace. There is one body, and one Spirit, even as ye are called in one hope of your calling; One Lord, one faith, one baptism. One God and Father of all, who is above all and through all and in you all. Ehp. 4:3-6

Gifts To The Church/Body of Christ:

And he gave some, apostles; and some, prophets; and some, evangelists; and some, pastors and teachers.

Purpose:

For the perfecting of the saints, for the work of the ministry, for the edifying of the body of Christ. Till we all come in the unity of the faith, and of the knowlege of the Son of God... Eph.4:11-13

PASTORS ARE "KEYHOLDERS" TO THE
"KINGDOM" OF GOD.

And I say also unto thee, That thou art "Peter," and upon this "rock" (Jesus)
I will build "my" "church;" and the gates of hell shall not prevail against
it. And "I" will give thee the "keys" to the "kingdom" of heaven; and
whatsoever thou shalt bind on earth shall be bound in heaven: and whatsoever
thou shalt loose on earth shall be loosed in heaven. Matt. 16:18-20
Bind—dictionary mean, to hold onto or hold together.
(heaven's record)
Loose—dictionary mean, unbound, untied, insecure, unattached, loosened,
diconnected, unlocked, loose oneself, unrestrained. ant-mean the opposite,
tight, confined, bound, release, (or turn) loose. (heaven's record).
...whatsoever a man soweth, that shall he also reap.
Galatians 6:7

ATTITUDES OF THE CHURCH

* US TWO AIN'T NOTHING TO DO

* US THREE WE'ER NOT FREE

* US FOUR AND NO MORE

* US FIVE CHURCH NOT ALIVE

* US SIX AND THE CHURCH IS SICK

* US SEVEN AND WE'ER ON OUR WAY TO HEAVEN

* US EIGHT WE ALWAYS LATE

* US NINE WE THINK WE'ER DOING FINE

* US TEN AND NO EVANGELISM CANT WIN

* US ELEVEN CHURCH TASTE LIKE WATER MELON

* US TWELVE NO REPENTANCE WE'ER ON OUR WAY TO HELL

Diagram

Theme: Scripture
Eph. 4:11 Acts 20:28 John 14:26
Holy Spirit - Teacher
Guide
Comforter

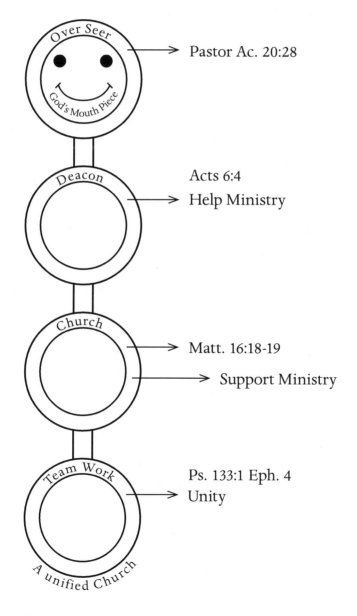

Pastor Ac. 20:28

Acts 6:4
Help Ministry

Matt. 16:18-19

Support Ministry

Ps. 133:1 Eph. 4
Unity

WORRIED TITHERS

Ps. 62:5; Mal. 3:8-10; Lk. 6:38; 1 Cor. 16:2; 2 Cor. 9:6-8

As a tither for over 35 years I was at least 22 years old when I start tithing I am now 57 years old. This is one of the most popular subjects in the church and in the secular world with so many different perspective.

Some people or tithers has too much pride to admit sometimes it is and can be a struggle along with paying other bills because we all srtuggle with having a persistent faith to maintain a good giving records.

I chose not to get into a debate over this matter because there is no Eternal Security rather we tithe or not our sure salvation and Eternal Security is only with a Relationship With Our Lord And Saviour Jesus Christ.

There some laity complained about their pastors preach more on this matter than any other sermons he preach. I have had many conversation among the clergyman who confess to me they do not tithe like they ought to and when this clergyman shared with me he don't tithe like he ought to his car or vehicles was in the shop the same day for repair over $ 800.00 work done to his car (Mal. 3:11)

This suject of tithes has had more teaching and training than teaching and training on the subject of "SALVATION" I have had many who confessed to be saved does not sound very sure of their salvation. The pulpit must do much better job of "TEACHING" THAN "WHOOPING" which is not a bibical term my friend and bible student pastor Patrick H.

Tisdale pastor of the Rehoboth Baptist Church in Jackson, Tn. shared with me the four gospel writers give reference to Jesus Christ teaching 89 times and preaching 11 times.

My experiences of giving more than enough of tithes has bless me and my family. I discovered many are giving God 10% but not the offerings I don't want to spend much time with explaining how tithes work when many been in church over 10 years or more and has never tithes. It is more of a faith problem than a money problem because both pastors and laity is more money-minded, and more-carnal minded, and more credit-minded and when we disobey God we become more misery-minded.

Tithers tithe without expecting blessing from God soon after the benediction people worry how they're going to pay bills those who don't tithe fear of getting behind on bills. ...for my expectation is from him (Ps. 62:5) ...if I will not open you the windows of heaven, and pour you out a blessing, there shall not be room enough to receive it (Mal. 3:9) Give...(Lk. 6:38) (obey) received the promises of God. Upon the first day of the week let every one of you (Body of Christ) lay by him in store, as God hath prospered him (...1 Cor. 16:2) And God is able to make all grace abound (overflow, plentiful) toward you (...2 Cor. 9:8). I have witness many worshipers on their way to church at the convenience store scratching lottery tickets.

Worship is incomplete from God perspective the five elements for worship is the following: 1. Prayer 2. Preaching 3. Teaching 4. Singing 5. Giving. We should always talk to God first before we talk to Man (Lk. 18:1) We must hear the preaching because So then faith cometh by hearing, and hearing by the word of God (Ro. 10:17) We must be at Sunday School and Bible Study to received Teaching ...let us wait on our ministering: or he that teacheth, on teaching (Ro. 12:7) We worship God with our singing ...come before his presence with singing (Ps. 100:2) We sing you can't beat God giving no matter how hard you try (Give... Lk. 6:38)

Ye worship ye know not what: we know what we worship: for salvation is of the Jews (John 4:22) But the hour is cometh, and now is, when the true worshippers shall worship the Father in spirit and in truth: for the Father seeketh such (of this kind, of that kind, such a person, accordingly, of the degree, so much) (tithers) to worship me (John 4:23) God is Spirit: and they that worship him must (requirement, need, obligation, necessity, ought) worship him in spirit (human) and in truth (John 4:24)

The Purpose of the tithes in The Old Testament was for the priest and his family first (Nu. 18:9-19) The purpose of the tithes and offerings in the New Testament is for the "Pastors" first the tithes is to take total care of the "Pastors" 110% ...for the workman is worthy of his meat (food) (Matt. 10:10) ...thou shalt not muzzle the mouth of the ox that treadeth out the corn (1 Cor. 9:9) If we have sown unto you spiritual things (THE WORD OF GOD) Is it a great thing if we shall reap your carnal things (MONEY, Gifts) (1 Cor. 9:11) Let the elders that rule well be counted worthy of double honour, especially they who labour in the word and doctrine (1 Tim. 5:17).

There are some Pastors may not "fit" the the scriptures because they go all year and not love on the people such as visit the sick, poor quality relationship with the people in the church, poor quality teaching, poor quality preaching, some pastors never spend quality time God, never have bible study, no christian education (1 Tim. 3:16) Some pastors never love on the people or congregation and expect a "Love Day Celebration Anually."

The black churches structure has never been healthy for total care for a pastor because of poor quality tradition mindset of the black churches we has never believed in taking care (Black Baptist Churches from a Black Perspective not from God Perspectives has not embrace this ministry.

The white churches is structure different from black churches because of their tradition mindset to take good care of their pastor (Acts 6:4) many of our churches has the financial stability. The tithes and offering is to finance the Kingdom of God the pastors hold the keys to the kingdom of God, And I say unto thee, That thou art Peter, and upon this rock I will build my church: and the gates of hell shall not prevail aganist it: And I WILL GIVE UNTO THEE THE KEYS of the kingdom of heaven (....Matt. 16:18-19)

The deacons hold the keys to the building (Haggai 1:1-5) (Ps. 24:1) (Acts 6:4) (1 Cor. 4:2) (1 Tim. 3:8-16) The pastors open the doors of the church the deacons open doors of the building. All deacons and all leaders of the church should tithe. All tithers don't always make good leaders and all leaders don't always make good tithers.

What make a good leader in the home also makes a good leader in the church and in the community (Joshua 24:15) The tithes is also is used to take care of God's property Ps. 24:1) (Haggai 1:1-5) tithes is also used for Hardship or Crisis in the life of the Believer in the Church (John 16:33) tithes is also used for compensate some church administration assistant staff. Tithes and Offering is used for Revivals, Leadership Training/Evangelism, Church Family Picnic, Out Reach Ministry, Benevolence (kindness) Tithes and Offerings is Used to Purchase Communion Juice, Tithes and offering is used for musicians, lawn service, Janitorial, secretary, maintenace, Radio and T.V. Ministry.

A faithful and true tither is going to make sure his or her tithes get to church when they are not going to be at church a tither should received Aide or Help from the church in case of hardship or crisis much more than a non-tither (Gal. 6:7-10) Tithers does not always have to pay this money back more so than a non-tither.

Many non-tithers money is tied up in cell phones, salon, weave, nails, make up, tectudes, car notes, eat-out, party, drink alcohol, house-notes, expensive rims for car, shopping, tunica missippi, lottery tickets, funerals, the church is not a utility bill headquarters nor a burial head quarters for uninsured indivdual the church is a soul-saving head head quarters. ...I pray not for the world (John 17:9) A non-tither should at least give God a thanksgiving and praise offering.

The main reason many fail to tithe, Lay not up for yourselves treasures upon earth (... Matt. 7:19) But lay up for yourselves treasures in heaven (...Matt. 7:20) For the love of money is the root of all evil (...1 Tim. 6:10) Tithes were before the law we all know that. The reasons some pastors never take a day off from the pulpit sometimes the offering drop when members know the pastor is not going to preach. A pastor shared his experience one Sunday from the pulpit offering drop from $17,000.00 to $ 9,000.00 he later discovered most in attendance was visitors he was a newly elected pastor.

I remember when I was out of the pulpit a few Sundays to give my brother a stem-cell transplant in Jacksonville, Fl. offering drop from $980.00 to $ 180.00. (small membership or large membership it don't matter)

Worried tithers must TRUST GOD not the tithes or money but God: both laity and pastors believe, And all things, whatsoever ye shall ask in prayer, believing, ye shall receive (Matt. 21:22) Have Faith In God (Mk. 11:22) Now unto him that is able to do exceeding abundantly (John 10:10) above all that we ask or think, according to the power (obedient faith) that worketh in us (Ehp. 3:20) But without faith it is impossible to please him: for he that cometh to God must believe that he is, and that he is a rewarder of them that diligently (hard work) seek him (Heb. 11:6).

We all need that mustard seed faith to move mountains we need a faith to move us from poverty to provisions and prosperity. Things seems impossible until it's done. Faith makes things possible not easy. Faith may guide you when you cannot see. May hope comfort you when you need it most. May you believe at all times...Trut in him at all times...(Ps. 62:8) When it is hardest to pray, pray the hardest. The struggle is real but my faith is stronger.

THINGS ARE GOING TO GET BETTER, HELP IS RIGHT AROUND THE CORNER "CHRIST" OUR KING, OUR LORD, OUR SAVIOUR, NEVER LEAVES US NOR FORSAKE US (Heb. 13:5) F.F.F.F.F.F Faith, Family, Future, Forever, Finish, Fight THE GOOD FIGHT OF FAITH... (1 TIM. 6:12).

SOME COMMEMTS OF THE CONGREGATION

the process of calling a pastor to a vacant church

1. What's taking God so long to send us a Pastor?
2. We wish we had took better care of our Pastor?
3. When the church say Amen to our Pastor?
4. We lost our Pastor of a tenure: 10 yrs. 15yrs. 21yrs. (lack of benefits)
5. We should feel our pastor and wife burdens or needs.
6. One day without a pastor is too long.
7. We must be on one accord and very prayerful for our pastor.
8. We want a God-Sent and God Fearing pastor.
9. We as the church should always help the man of God with responsibilities around the church.
10. We must be a giving and loving church.
11. We must forgive our pastor for all of his mistakes.
12. We must let our pastor pastor the church.
13. We thank God for our spirit-filled, spirit-fed, and spirit-led pastor.
14. We thank God the Father, God the Son, God the Holy Spirit for our pastor.
15. The Holy Spirit made the pastor overseer not pulpit committee.
16. God left the Holy Spirit in charge of the church.
17. The Holy Spirit is the most important person on earth.
18. The church can operate without organizations but not without a pastor (deacons, musicians, janitor, trustee, usher, etc.)
19. Is there ever time we need a pastor we need one right now and daily.
20. We need pastor/word for our aching pain.

21. We need our pastor to visit our children in jail.
22. We need counseling for our teenage daughter pregnancy.
23. We need our pastor visit the hospital and nursing home.
24. We need our pastor to preach the gospel of Jesus Christ.
25. We need a pastor who loves pastoring more than preaching.

PASTOR'S COMPENSATION/STRAGETY

The pastor and the congregation must have good working relationship with one another to compensate and or negotiate a good benefit package.

Negotiate-make peace, contract, make the best, agreement, discussion. The church and pastor can agree on the following: "Breathing Room" (Options)

1. Pastor keep a low paid salary.
2. Church pays half or all house note.
3. Church pay half or all cell phone bill.
4. Church pay half or all utility bill.
5. Church make "Budget" for Pastor and his Family.
6. Church help with half or all medical expenses.
7. Church celebrate "Pastor's National Day
8. Church celebrate Pastor's Appreciation Day

Appreciate mean (to be grateful, welcome, pay respects to, be indebted, feel or be obligated, acknowledge, never forget, overflow with gratitude, to reconize worth, esteem, honor, praise, admire, like.

Appreciation mean (sense of gratitude, thankfulness, recognition, gratefulness, (Favorable Opinion) esteem, high regard, enjoyment, appreciativeness, love, affection senitivity,

Appreciative mean thankful, appreciatory, indebted, cooperative, aware, favorable, satisfied, considerate, friendly kindly, gladdened. Ant. opposite: unfriendly, cold, hostile.

9. Church pay half or all vacation.
10. Church pay all expenses of Christian Edcation: College, Leadership Training (Seminars, Workshops, etc.)
11. Church pay half or all Wardrode cleaning (Suits, shirts, etc.)
12. Church have "Book Budget" to purchase books to study.
13. Church pay half or all car note.

The Church Cannot do enough for God's Anointed One, God's Chosen Vessel, God's Servants, The Man of God, The Angel of God's Bride, God' Shepherd/Under Shepherd.

For God is not unrighteous to forget your work and labour of love, which ye shewed toward his name, in that ye have ministered to the saints, and do minister (Heb. 6:10)

And to esteem them very highly in love for their work's sake. And at peace among yourselves (1 Thess. 5:13)

These strageties can help the pastors devote himself with spending "Quality Time" WITH THE MASTER (Acts 6:4).

WE LOVE OUR PASTOR

Process of calling a pastor to a vacant pulpit God's Will, Way, Word.

Benefits of God's Pulpit/Preacher/Pastor/Prayer/Purposed.

We thank God for our pastor's:

1. Prayers 2. Preaching 3. Teaching 4. Lectures 5. Counseling 6. Wedding 7. Funerals 8. Love 9. Hospitality 10. Support 11. Anointing 12. Sense of humor 13. Attitude 14. Personality 15. Love 16. Spirituality 17. Concerns 18. Considerate 19. Tither 20. Faith 21. Faithfulness 22. Sunday School 23. Bible Study 24. Tenure 25. Grace 26. Mercy 27. Visionary 28. Prayerfulness 29. Cares 30. Persistent 31. Plans 32. God-Sent 33. Leadership 34. Relationship 35. Fellowship 36. Forgiven 37. Spirit-Filled 38. Listen 39. Learn 40. Life-Style 41. Salvation 42. Truth 43. Intelligence 44. Timely Sermons 45. Sound Doctrine 46. Commitment 47. Devoted 48. Dedicated 49. Rightly-Divided/Word 50. Appreciation.

Pastors Leadership Prayer

O Lord I am thankful and grateful for your divine alignment for your divine assignment. Thank you for all my trials, tribulations (Jn. 16:33). O Lord I must continue remind myself you are the owner and operator of the church and she cannot function without you (Jn. 15:5) O Lord help me allow the Holy Spirit trained me be the administrator and overseer of your heritage being example to the flock. According to scriptures the term CEO Chief Executive Officer is not what the Holy Spirit mention in scriptures:

Take heed therefore unto yourselves, and to all the flock, over which the Holy Ghost hath made you overseers (not CEO'S) to feed the church (WORD) of God, which he had purchased with his own (BLOOD) (Acts 20:28). O Lord help me trained men/deacons to know their duties and responsibilities from a biblcal perspective.

I am experiencing afflictions (1 Thess. 3:3) and struggle with the Archenemy (satan) Father God many despiseth, despiseth not man, but God, who hath also given unto us his holy Spirit (1 Thess. 3:8). Father God you has allowed this your servant to be put in trust with the gospel, even so we speak: not as pleasing men, but God, which trieth (test) our hearts (1 Thess. 2:4). O Lord give this your servant guidance and direction to lead your sheeps (Pr. 3:5-6). O Lord help me to be a motivator leader motivating your people to paritcipate and co-operate and take an interest and support every function of the church.

O Lord you said, He that heareth you hearth me: and he that despiseth you despiseth me: and he hath despiseth me despiseth him that sent me (Lk. 9:16). O Lord you said...the harvest is truly is plenteous, but the labours are few: Pray ye therefore the Lord of the harvest, that he will send forth labours into his harvest (Matt. 9:37-38).

Heavenly Father bless me with visions and goals to accomplished the divine assignment. Father I pray we all be ready when Jesus come (Jn. 14:1-4).

O Lord I have a desire to continue this assignment or accept another one according to your will. O Lord, in spite what problems we have had: I will bless the Lord at all times: his praise shall continue be in my mouth. My soul shall make her boast in the Lord: the humble shall hear thereof, and be glad. O magnify the Lord with me, and let us exalt his name together. O taste and see that the Lord is good: blessed is the man that trusted in him (Psa. 34:1,2,3,8).

O Lord I believe things are going to get better: For his anger endureth but a moment: in his favor is life: weeping may endure for, but joy cometh in the morning (Psa. 30:5). O Lord I pray these souls have eternal life: And this is life eternal, that they might know thee the only true God, and Jesus Christ whom thou has sent (Jn. 17:3).

Heavenly Father: I pray that you bless me to be faithful over those you has given me the ability to served: His lord said unto him, Well done, thou good and faithful servant: thou has been faithful over a few things, I will make thee ruler over many things: enter thou into the joy of thy lord (Matt. 25:21).

Father God thank you for many souls you saved under my watch: Likewise, I say unto you, there is joy in the presence of God over one sinner that repenteth (Lk. 15:10). In the name of Jesus Christ. Amen.

FIRST LADY PRAYER

Heavenly Father thank you for calling me to be a help meet (Gn. 2:18) to my husband as he care for your people (2 Chr. 7:14). Heavenly Father I pray you will help me to be clothed with the garment of salvation and covered with the robe of righteousness, as a bridegroom decked himself with ornaments, as a bride adorneth herself with her jewels (Isa. 61:10).

Heavenly Father help me be a virtuous woman to my husband both through good and evil and he will trust me as his help meet all the days of his life and provide for our family both night and day. Heavenly Father I pray as my husband help meet I will help the needy and be his covering and honour him in our home and the church as well in the community. I pray as the spiritual-mother of the church I will speak with wisdom. I pray my children and my husband recognized the blessings in our lives and help me to continue to be a God fearing wife and first lady to my husband ministry (Pr. 31:10-31).

Dear Lord I pray for strenght and good courage (Josh. 1:6) to fulfilled my role as first lady I pray you will help me keep the doors of my mouth (Psa. 141:3) and pray without ceasing (1 Thess. 5:17). I pray our Father help me reframe from burnouts of overcommitment from this ministry (1 Ki. 19:4). I pray for my husband daily to be the servant of God and man of God to his family and to make sound decision for his family and the congregation (Pr. 3:5-6). Father I pray for other first ladies as you said bear one another burdens (Gal. 6:2) and I ask your forgiveness for my slackness (1 Jn. 1:9).

Dear Lord I realized this is not my husband church but yours (Jer. 3:15) you only have made him overseer (Acts 20:28) and because my husband is pastor he must know how to rule his own house, and take care of the church of God (1 Tim. 3:5). Father God help me to be a kingdom minded (Matt. 6:33) and christ minded (Phil. 2:5) wife and first lady to my husband. Dear Lord you said, let the elders that rule well be counted worthy of double honour, especially they who labour in the word and doctrine. Lord continue to help my husband labour in your word and doctrine (1 Tim. 3:17).

Dear Lord you said, All scriptures is given by inspiration of God, and his profitable for doctrine, for reproof, for correction, for instruction in righteousness: That the man of God may be perfect throughly furnished unto all good works (2 Tim. 3:16) Lord I pray you keep my husband humble and prayerful through out his tenure as pastor and his divine assignment. Dear Lord I pray in the name of Jesus Christ (Jn. 14:14) I pray you will allow my husband and family time together (Psa. 133:1). In Jesus name. Amen.

DEACONS ARE "KEYHOLDERS" TO THE BUILDING

Then the twelve called the multitude of the disciples unto them, and
said, it is not reason that we should leave the word of God, and serve
tables. ...whom we may appoint over this business. But we will give ourselves
continually to prayer, and to the ministry of the word. Acts 6:2-4

Moreover it is required in stewards, that a man be found faithful. 1 Cor. 4:2

And let these also first be proved: 1 Tim. 3:10

...ruling their children and their own houses well.

1 Tim. 3:12

The earth is the Lord's...Psa. 24:1

It is time for you, O ye, to dwell in your cieled houses,
and this house lie waste. Haggai 1:4

Model-Minded, Christ-Minded, Mission-Minded, Kingdom-Minded

Faith-Driven, Shred It!

Model-minded

To model is to imitate, duplicate, or to served as an example in the community. The New Testament church model the leadership style of Jesus Christ through The Acts of the Apostles chapter 2:41-47. They gladly received his word and were baptized some of today's churches is gladly receiving the word and is baptized but it seem as though the body of Christ is not continuing stedfast or faithful in the Sunday School, and Bible Study as well as other chrisian education activities v. 44 and all that believed were together, and had all things common v.46 and they, continuing daily with one accord in the temple (Heb. 10:25) The African-American church tradition mindset is v. 46 is to break bread during annual days which does not model the model church.

To be Christ-Minded (Phil. 2:5) is a mind to please his heavenly Father.

I can of mine own self do nothing: asl hear, I judge: and my judgment is just: because I seek not mine own will, but the will of the Father which hath sent me (Jn. 5:30). I received not honour from men (Jn. 5:41) At that day ye shall know that I am in my Father, and ye in me, and I in you (Jn. 14:20). Paul also and Barnabas continued in Antioch, teaching and preaching the word of the Lord, with many others also (Acts 15:35).

Mission-Minded: To be mission-minded is to know our purpose. Go ye therefore, and teach all nations, baptizing them in the name of the Father, and of the Son, and of the Holy

Ghost. Teaching them to observed all things whatsoever I have commanded you: and, lo, I am with you alway, even unto the end of the world (Matt. 28:19-20).

Kingdom-Minded: To be kingdom-minded is to seek the kingdom of God first and his righteousness: and all these things shall be added unto you (Matt. 6:33)

Faith-Purpose- Driven: Everything we do for the Lord must be to please God. Now faith is the substance of things hoped for, the evidence of things not seen. But without faith it is impossible to please him: for he that cometh to God must believe that he is, and that he is a rewarder of them that diligently seek him (Heb. 11:1, 6) Faith must drive us to our destiny.

Shred It: mean to tear, strip, cut into small pieces. There are some habits we must get rid of to call a pastor to an vacant pulpit. We must shred our tradition mindset by forgetting those things which are behind, and reaching forth unto those things which are before. I press toward the mark for the prize of the high calling of God in Christ Jesus (Phil. 3:13-14).

TOPICS

Control Aniexty—Eph. 5:18

Breathing Room—Mal. 3:8-10

Good Communicator—Heb. 13:16

Look for God in Ministry—Eph. 5:17

Stay Focus—Phil. 3:13

Avoid Pitfall—Ps. 23:2,3; Pr. 3:5-6; Ps. 37:23; Jer. 10:23

Learn Your Lessons—Jas. 1:5

Trust God's Assignment—Jer. 3:15

Right Perspective—Isa. 55:8-9

God the Father—Gn. 1:1

God the Son—Jn. 3:16

God the Holy Spirit—Jn. 14:26

God's Purpose—Jer. 29:11

God's Ministry—Matt; Mk; Lk; Jn.

God's Church—Matt. 16:18

Financial Family Meeting/F.F.M.—Josh. 24:15

Proper Perspective of Prayer/P.P.P.—Lk. 18:1; 1 Thess. 5:17

Prepared to Praise God—Pr. 16:1

The Battle Is Not Yours—2 Chr. 20:15,17

No Short-Cuts With God—Jn. 15:5

Expect God's Deliverance—Psa. 62:5

Expect More From God—Jn. 10:10

Be Still and Wait On God—Psa. 46:10

Family Prays Together—Eph. 5:22-23; 6:1-4

Church Prays Together—Acts 12:7-19

Never Negotiate Salvation—Acts 4:12

We Fall Down, But We Get Up—Jn. 16:33; Phil. 4:13

God The Restorer Of My Soul—Psa. 23:3

God In The Valley With You—Psa. 23:4

God In The Cave With You—1 Ki. 19:9,12

God In The Fiery Furnance With You—Dan. 3:19-25

God In The Lion's Den With You—Dan. 6:16-20

God in The Storm With You—Lk. 8:22-25

Salvation In Christ—2 Cor. 5:17

Grave Could Not Hold Him—Matt:28:16-20; Mk. 16:1-9; Lk. 24:1-12; Jn. 20:1-10.

Pastor and Temptation

Temptation (bait, attraction, appeal) temptation itself is not temptation. It is when we become tempted (diserious. seduced, enticed, wish to enjoy)

My brethren, count it all joy when you fall into divers temptation (Jas. 1:2)

There is no temptation taken you but as is common to man: but God is faithful, who will not suffer you to be tempted above ye are able; but will with the temptation also make a way to escape, that ye may be able to bear it (1 Cor. 10:13)

Sometimes we all can put ourselves in a position to fulfilled the lust of our flesh...Walk in the Spirit, and ye shall not fulfil the lust of the flesh (Ga. 5:16)

(For the weapons of our warfare are not carnal, but mighty through God to the pulling down of strong holds;) Casting down imaginations, and every high thing that exalted itself against the knowledge of God, and bringing into captivity every thought to the obedience of Christ (2 Cor. 10:4-5)

The temptation of Potiphar wife and Joseph, And it came to pass after these things, that his master's wife cast eyes upon Joseph and said, Lie with me (Gen. 39:7)

But he refused...(Gen. 39:8)

Joesph ran from temptation but David ran to temptation.

And it came to pass in an eveningtide, that David arose from off his bed, walked upon the roof of the king's house: and from the roof he saw a woman washing herself; and the woman was very beautiful to look upon (2 Sam. 10:2) And David sent and enquired after the woman...(2 Sam. 10:3) And David sent messengers, and took her; and she came in unto him, and he lay with her (2 Sam. 10:4) ... And the woman conceived, and sent and told David, and said, I am with child (2 Sam. 10:5)

And lead us not into temptation, but deliver us from evil...(Matt. 6:13)

There has been many pastors has lost some good churches because of temptation and sexual desires in the church.

BEWARE OF WASP

MENTALITY/INTELLECT

Nelson's Illustrated Bible Dictionary: Ronald F. Youngblood General Editor and F.F. Bruce & R.K. Harrison. Definition for Wasp/Dogs

Wasp is these overgrown relatives of bees are known for their painful sting. Wasps are common throughout the Holy Land. Hornets are a species of wash. So savage were these insects when disturbed that the Egyptian soldiers used hornets as a symbol of their military might. When the people of Israel were marching toward the Promised Land, God promised He would send hornets before them to drive the Canaanites out of the land (Ex. 23:28). Ancient writers claim that entire tribes were sometimes driven out of a country by wasps or hornets.

A few weeks ago my wife Vanessa was decorating for Christmas on the front porch of our home and inform me there were some wasp nest. When I went to remove them my wife warn me not to get stung/sting and I shared with her I only found two and we did not have any wasp insect spray so I use some bathroom cleaner to kill I thought only two wasp and when I sprayed the bathroom cleaner inside the wasp nest more than 25 wasps came out of the nest.

This is the way it is in life sometimes we think we only have two peoples or enemies do not like us. Sometimes we have more than 25 wasps in our own family, church, community, jobs, whitehouse, and somtimes even in your own homes, neighbors, etc.

When a vacant pulpit is searching for pastor without the guidance and direction and a intimate relationship with the Holy Spirit the church could possible preach 25 wasps mentality preachers who have no christian experience, no shepherd heart to be an effective pastor, he could be a hireling ...(John 10:12,13). Sometimes without the Holy Spirit (Acts 20:28) chosen the right candidate (wasps) overgrown species intellectual immature (2 Pt. 3:18) preachers/wasps can do much stinging and damaging to the pew with poor quality preaching, teaching, leadership training, can cause some painful decisions (Pr. 3:5-6) and short tenure. Sometimes God has some disgrumbled, anger, bitter, power control deacons, members, leaders to vote out the one he did not make the divine assignment and sometimes has to start the process all over again.

Beware of false prophets, which come to you in sheep's clothing, but inwardly they are ravening wolves, ye shall know them by their fruits...(Matt. 7:15-16). It is as many wasps (members) in the pew with a stinging mentality not willing to accept change from their tradition mindset But he answered and said unto them, Why do ye also transgress the commandment of God by your tradition (Matt. 15:3).

These wasps or hornets is in every congregation hid on the inside of the wasps nest (hearts of peoples) not only the pew but also the puplit/pastors/preachers/bishops/doctor degrees/P.H.D.'s/Master's Degrees/all denominations/all race, color, creed. For all have sinned, and come short of the glory of God (Ro. 3:23). Please beware of the Hornet nest may look like you have none or two when you spray your bathroom cleaner (The Holy Spirit).

O Lord, thou hast searched me, and known me. Thou knowest my downsitting and mine uprising, thou understandest my thought afar off. Thou compassest my path and my lying down, and art acquainted with all my ways. For there is not a word in my tongue, but, lo, O LORD, thou, knowest it altogether. Thou hast beset me behind and before, and laid thine hand upon me. Such knowledge is too wonderful for me: it is high, I cannot attain unto it. Whither shall I go from thy spirit? or whither shall I flee from thy presence? If I ascend into heaven, thou art there: if I make my bed in hell, behold, thou art there. If I take the wings of the morning, and dwell in the uttermost parts of the sea. Even there shall thy hand lead me, and thy right hand hold. If I say, Surely the darkness shall cover me: even the night shall be light about me. Yea, the darkness hideth not from thee: but the night shineth as the day: the darkness and the light are both alike to thee. For possessed my reins: thou hast covered me in my mother's womb. I will praise thee; for Iam fearfully and wonderfully made: marvellous are thy works; and that my soul knoweth right well. (Psa. 139:1-14).

My substance was not hid from thee, when I was made in secret, and curiously wrought in the lowest parts of the earth. Thine eyes did see my substance, yet being unperfect: and in thy book all my members were written... (Psa. 139:15-16)

Search me, O God, and know my heart: try me, and know my thoughts: And see if there be any wicked way in me, and lead me in the way everlasting. (Psa. 139:23-24).

And I will send hornets before thee, which shall drive out the Hiivite, and the Canaanite, and the Hitte, from before thee. I will not drive them out before thee in one year; least the land become desolate, and the beast of the field multiply against thee. By little and little I will drive them out from before thee, until thou be increased, and inherit the land (Ex. 23:27-30).

And daily in the temple, and in every house, they ceased not to teach and preach Jesus Christ (Acts 5:42).

And the word of God increased: and the number of the disciples multiplied in Jerusalem greatly; and a great company of the priests were obedient to the faith (Acts 6:7).

The Pastor Every Church Want

The Process of calling a pastor to a vacant pulpit

1. Quality Leadership 2. God Chose Him 3. God Anoint Him 4. God Appoint Him 5. God Orders Him 6. God Lead Him 7. God Keep Him 8. God Feed Him 9. God Spirit-Filled Him 10. God Take Care of Him 11. God Forgives Him 12. Guide Him 13. Direct Him 14. Total Submissive 15. Full-Time Service 16. Love Pastoring 17. Love People 18. Love Preaching 19. Love Teaching 20. Praying 21. Studious 22. Educated 23. Honest 24. Student of the Bible 25. Overseer 26. Watchman 27. Communicator 28. Sacrificial 29. Punctual 30. Decisived 31. Shepherding 32. Pull Me Out My Pit 33. Get A Prayer Through 34. Travel 35. After God's Heart 36. Saved 37. Born-Again 38. God's Alignment 39. God's Assignment 40. God-Fearing

How to Call a Pastor:
Prayer is Necessary for Calling a Pastor

The Church Must Pray

The whole Church must pray together for the calling of a pastor/undershepherd to serve under the guidance and direction of the Holy Spirit.

> The steps of a good man are ordered by the LORD: and he delighted in his way (Psalm 37:23).

> Trust in the Lord with all thine heart; and lean not unto thine own understanding. In all thy ways acknowledge him, and he shall direct thy paths (Proverbs 3:5-6).

> O Lord, I know that the way of man is not in himself: it is not in man that walketh to direct his steps (Jeremiah 10:23).

> Blessed is the man that walketh not in the counsel of the ungodly, nor standeth in the way of sinners, nor sit in the seat of the scornful (Psalm 1:1).

The Church should pray a prayer of thanksgiving, thanking God for the pastor, who has served out his tenure, and for all the good that was done under his watch.

The Church must come together for prayer and supplication asking God to give divine instructions and to elect the undershepherd/shepherd he chooses to be the overseer of this local congregation.

The Church must acknowledge who the Church belongs to.

> And I say also unto thee, That thou art Peter, and upon this rock I will build my church; and the gates of hell shall not prevail against it (Matt. 16:18).

The Church must pray like the model Church prayed for Peter when he was in prison.

> And when he had considered the thing, he came to the house of Mary the mother of John, whose surname was Mark; where many were gathered together praying (Acts 12:12).

> The Scripture says, "And he spake a parable unto them to this end, that men ought always to pray and not faint" (Luke 18:1).

The Church must fast and pray becoming more sensitive to the voice of the Holy Spirit.

> And there was one Anna, a prophetess, the daughter of Phanuel, of the tribe of Aser: she was of a great age, and had lived with an husband seven years from her virginity; And she was a widow of about fourscore and four years, which departed not from the temple, but served God with fastings and prayers night and day (Luke 2:36-37).

> Jesus said unto him, if thou canst believe, all things are possible to him that believeth (Mark 9:23).

Prayer and fasting bring us into the awareness and presence of the Holy Spirit.

> Wherefore (as the Holy Ghost saith, To day if ye will hear his voice, Harden not your hearts, as in the provocation, in the day of temptation in the wilderness (Hebrews 3:7-8)

The Church must pray according to the Scriptures,

> Ask, and it shall be given you; seek, and ye shall find; knock, and it shall be opened unto you. For every one that asketh receiveth; and he that seeketh findeth; and to him that knocketh it shall be opened (Matt. 7:7-8).

When a Church calls a pastor, the Church must pray for guidance and courage to delete some traditions that may be a hindrance to the body of Christ.

Then came to Jesus scribes and Pharisees, which were of Jerusalem, saying, Why do thy disciples transgress the tradition of the elders? for they wash not their hands when they eat bread. But he answered and said unto them, Why do ye also transgress the commandment of God by your tradition? For God commanded, saying, Honour thy father and mother: and, He that curseth father or mother, let him die the death. But ye say, Whosoever shall say to his father or his mother, It is a gift, by whatsoever thou mightest be profited by me; And honour not his father or his mother, he shall be free. Thus have ye made the commandment of God of none effect by your tradition. Ye hypocrites, well did Esaias prophesy of you, saying, This people draweth nigh unto me with their mouth, and honoureth me with their lips; but their heart is far from me. But in vain they do worship me, teaching for doctrines the commandments of men. And he called the multitude, and said unto them, Hear, and understand: Not that which goeth into the mouth defileth a man; but that which cometh out of the mouth, this defileth a man. Then came his disciples, and said unto him, Knowest thou that the Pharisees were offended, after they heard this saying? But he answered and said, Every plant, which my heavenly Father hath not planted, shall be rooted up. Let them alone: they be blind leaders of the blind. And if the blind lead the blind, both shall fall into the ditch. Then answered Peter and said unto him, Declare unto us this parable. And Jesus said, Are ye also yet without understanding? Do not ye yet understand, that whatsoever entereth in at the mouth goeth into the belly, and is cast out into the draught? But those things which proceed out of the mouth come forth from the heart; and they defile the man. For out of the heart proceed evil thoughts, murders, adulteries, fornications, thefts, false witness, blasphemies: These are the things which defile a man: but to eat with unwashen hands defileth not a man (Matt. 15:1-20).

There are some things the Church must do prior to calling a pastor to lead the congregation. Even our Lord and Savior prayed before he chose his twelve apostles.

And it came to pass in those days, that he went out into a mountain to pray, and continued all night in prayer to God. And when it was day, he called unto him his disciples; and of them he chose twelve whom also he named apostles (Luke 6:12-13).

There must be a time of personal prayer as our Lord and Savior Jesus Christ demonstrated in the Scriptures.

> And in the morning, rising up a great while before day, he went out and departed into a solitary place, and there prayed (Mark 1:35).

> And straightway Jesus constrained his disciples to get into a ship, and to go before him unto the other side, while he sent the multitudes away. And when he had sent the multitudes away, he went up into a mountain apart to pray: and when the evening was come, he was there alone (Matt. 14:22-23).

There must be a prayer of supplication; be specific to God on what kind of pastor you would like to be your undershepherd.

> The Scriptures teach us in Philippians, "Be careful for nothing: but in everything by prayer and supplication with thanksgiving let your requests be made known unto God" (Philippians 4:6).

Jesus Christ prayed a prayer of supplication in the gospel of John Chapter 17. In verses 1-5, he prayed for himself. In verses 6-19, he prayed for his disciples. In verses 20-26, he prayed for believers who would believe through the word of the disciples.

There must be ongoing, persistent prayer requests and supplication in corporate prayer meetings on a daily and weekly schedule for God to act and move upon the body of Christ and for him to fulfill this divine assignment within a timely manner.

The Scriptures according to 1 Timothy 2:1-6 teach,

> I exhort therefore, that, first of all, supplications, prayers, intercessions, and giving of thanks, be made for all men; For kings, and for all that are in authority; that we may lead a quiet and peaceable life in all godliness and honesty. For this is good and acceptable in the sight of God our Saviour; Who will have all men to be saved, and to come unto the knowledge of the truth. For there is one God, and one mediator between God and men, the man Christ Jesus; Who gave himself a ransom for all, to be testified in due time (1 Timothy 2:1-6).

The prayer for a pastor ought to be a prayer of requests and supplication asking God for a saved, born again, Holy Spirit-filled, and trained by the Holy Spirit pastor to train the body of Christ or the Church.

Prayers of supplications are asking God for a leader with visions, goals, and ideas to move the Church forward, which include a persistent leadership training program and a persistent prayer meeting on a regular basis.

When the Church calls a pastor, the Church must keep him lifted in prayer daily for courage, strength, and divine guidance and direction that will bring glory to Almighty God.

God honors unity in the Church,

> "For where two or three are gathered together in my name, there am I in the midst of them" (Matt. 18:20).

> Behold, how good and how pleasant it is for brethren to dwell together in unity! (Psalm 133:1).

How to Call a Pastor:
The Interim Minister

The interim pastor or minister can consist of the associate minister or the vacant church can agree to have a minister from another church serve as their pulpit supply.

The interim pastor has no authority to make decisions for the church, unless the Church agrees with the decision.

The interim pastor can perform communion, funerals, weddings, and other events needed by the church, only if he has been ordained and if the Church agrees.

The interim pastor is not in position to ordain any deacons or associate minister because that is the responsibility of the pastor who will be assigned by God to that congregation.

The interim pastor may be considered by the vacant church as the elected pastor if the Church agrees to it.

The Church must keep the interim pastor informed of when a candidate is scheduled to preach on a certain Sunday. The Church must also inform the interim pastor that he may or may not be elected as their pastor.

The interim pastor has the right to visit the sick, the shut-in, and bereaved families, but he is not obligated to do so as the interim pastor.

The interim pastor must inform the Church if he is a candidate for another church. The interim pastor must also give the vacant church notice if he is not going to be able to serve on a certain Sunday.

How to Call a Pastor: Ministerial Compensation

Salary

One of the major considerations in the process of calling a pastor is the salary to be offered. Foremost, we must realize that person is a professional like any other profession, such as a doctor, lawyer, dentist, etc.

The pastor deals with "spiritual" matters, so there are some situations to take into consideration, such as education, seminary training, and college degree. We must also consider what is the average salary paid to head of household in the congregation.

Scripture teaches us in 1 Timothy 5:17-18,

Let the elders that rule well be counted worthy of double honour; especially they who labour in the word and doctrine. For the Scripture saith, Thou shalt not muzzle the ox that treadeth out the corn. And the labourer is worthy of his reward.

The church must take into consideration the distance the pastor has to travel to and from the church. The church must also consider a salary and benefit package to compensate him as the full-time non-bi-vocational pastor.

The pastor and the church must have an understanding with one another about his benefit package. The church should also have a Pastor and Wife Appreciation or Love Day. The pastor can have a base salary and still have appreciation.

Library Budget

The church should allow the pastor a book or literature budget to purchase books and other related materials to help the pastor become more advanced in the work of the ministry.

All churches must budget according to the size of their membership, as well as evaluate the church's income, outcome, and the needs of their pastor and his family.

The church should compensate their pastor with love and respect, as well as pray that his tenure will be enjoyable and rewarding to his life-long career.

Related Expenses

The church should consider providing compensation for mileage expenses while performing church business.

The pastor should attend all district, state, and national levels of conventions which the church is registered, and the church should provide compensation for all the pastor's expenses. These functions will keep the pastor informed of Christian education and will equip the pastor with learning skills, growth, and development opportunities to be an effective leader of the congregation.

There should also be funds available in the budget to continue the pastor's education at the church's expense.

The Baptist Church Covenant paragraph number two states: "to contribute cheerfully and regularly to the support of the ministry, the *expenses* of the church, the relief of the poor, and the spread of the gospel through all nations."

HOW TO CALL A PASTOR:
INSTALLING A PASTOR

The installation service is to officially put a newly elected pastor in position or in place to serve as the undershepherd of the local congregation for an indefinite period of tenure.

The installation service revenues or all money or monies raised should be given to the newly elected pastor and his family, according to what the church agrees on.

Some churches give both the morning and evening revenues, and some churches give one of the service offerings.

The installation service should be done within a timely manner. The newly elected pastor has the right to choose who he wants to install him.

HOW TO CALL A PASTOR: PULPIT COMMITTEE

The Process of Calling a Pastor

The purpose of the pulpit committee is to keep order and structure in the local church. The pulpit committee also makes recommendation to the congregation on the candidate they feel would be a good and competent leader and an asset for the church.

The pulpit committee and the Church must understand that God makes the divine assignment for the overseer of the congregation according to the following Scriptures.

> And I will give you pastors according to mine heart, which shall feed you with knowledge and understanding (Jeremiah 3:15)

> So when they had dined, Jesus saith to Simon Peter, Simon, son of Jonas, lovest thou me more than these? He saith unto him, Yea, Lord; thou knowest that I love thee. He saith unto him, Feed my lambs. He saith to him again the second time, Simon, son of Jonas, lovest thou me? He saith unto him, Yea, Lord; thou knowest that I love thee. He saith unto him, Feed my sheep. He saith unto him the third time, Simon, son of Jonas, lovest thou me? Peter was grieved because he said unto him the third time, Lovest thou me? And he said unto him, Lord, thou knowest all things; thou knowest that I love thee. Jesus saith unto him, Feed my sheep (John 21:15-17).

> Take heed therefore unto yourselves, and to all the flock, over the which the Holy Ghost hath made you overseers, to feed the church of God, which he hath purchased with his own blood (Acts 20:28).

> The elders which are among you I exhort, who am also an elder, and a witness of the sufferings of Christ, and also a partaker of the glory that shall be revealed: Feed the flock of God which is among you, taking the

oversight thereof, not by constraint, but willingly; not for filthy lucre, but of a ready mind (1 Peter 5:1-2).

The pulpit committee must prayerfully select those who will make a sound decision for the church.

> Wherefore, brethren, look ye out among you seven men of honest report, full of the Holy Ghost and wisdom, whom we may appoint over this business (Acts 6:3).

The pulpit committee must prayerfully consider and process resumes of both experienced and inexperienced candidates. A candidate does not have to be ordained to be considered or elected as a pastor, but he must be ordained to serve as a pastor.

Through much prayer and supplication of the Church, it is very important that the church does not have an extended amount of time of candidates. Try not to have a preaching contest; be sensitive and follow the guidance of the Holy Spirit.

> Trust in the Lord with all thine heart; and lean not unto thine own understanding. In all thy ways acknowledge him, and he shall direct thy paths (Proverbs 3:5-6).

The pulpit committee should allow the candidates to preach, teach Sunday school, and teach Bible class to get an idea of his theology and doctrine.

> Study to shew thyself approved unto God, a workman that needeth not to be ashamed, rightly dividing the word of truth (2 Timothy 2:15).

When calling a pastor, you must take into consideration that an untrained pulpit and an untrained pew can create problems. The Holy Spirit is the one who trains the pulpit, and the pulpit trains the pew. The pulpit and the pew both must have a teachable and trainable spirit in order for the Church to grow and develop into a healthy church.

The pulpit committee has a responsibility to know what kind of leader the church is looking for so that they can make the recommendation. Sometimes, the church predecessor can name or appoint his successor if the church agrees on the recommendation of the predecessor. Then, there would be no need for a pulpit committee.

> After these things the Lord *appointed* other seventy also and sent them two and two before his face into every city and place wither he himself would come (Luke 10:1).

> Wherefore brethren, look ye put among you seven men of honest report, full of the Holy Ghost, and wisdom, whom we may *appoint* over this business (Acts 6:3).

The question has been asked how long should a pulpit be vacant or without a pastor? No more than twenty-four hours. Why? In the Bible, sheep are mentioned frequently, about 750 times. When calling a pastor, you call him to be a shepherd as God was to Israel. Figuratively, the Old Testament pictures God as Israel's Shepherd.

> Give ear, O Shepherd of Israel, thou that leadest Joseph like a flock; thou that dwellest between the cherubims, shine forth (Psalm 80:1).

The reason this vacancy must be filled only by the Holy Spirit as soon as possible is because the New Testament reveals Jesus as the Good Shepherd who gave his life for His sheep. Sheep cannot survive without a Shepherd. In the natural, David fed the sheep every morning with fresh grass and water to nurture their hungry bodies.

> He maketh me to lie down in green pastures: he leadeth me beside the still waters (Psalm 23:2).

In the spiritual realm, a person or the body of Christ will suffer from spiritual malnutrition without a pastor/shepherd/undershepherd/leader. The pastor-shepherd must be considered prayerfully and carefully.

A person can preach without pastoring, but he cannot pastor without preaching. The pulpit committee must be sensitive to the voice of the Holy Spirit.

> And after the earthquake a fire; but the Lord was not in the fire: and after the fire a still small voice (1 Kings 19:12).

Be still, and know that I am God: I will be exalted among the heathen, I will be exalted in the earth. The Lord of hosts is with us; the God of Jacob is our refuge. Selah (Psalm 46:10-11).

The pulpit committee must be mindful to trust God to elect a pastor who will be able to keep peace and harmony with the congregation.

Blessed are the peacemakers: for they shall be called the children of God (Matt. 5:9).

The pulpit committee must write down questions about the candidate during the interview. Also, it is not good policy for any church to advertise in the newspaper or to use any secular method for searching for a pastor.

The church is a spiritual organism, not an organization. The church or the body of Christ must seek God through much prayer and supplication to fill the vacancy of the pulpit. The Church should not turn to the world for kingdom business. The Church is God's business, and the Scripture says,

But seek ye first the kingdom of God, and his righteousness: and all these things will be added unto you (Matt. 6:33).

Behold, I am the Lord, the God of all flesh: is there anything too hard for me? (Jeremiah 32:27).

Call unto me, and I will answer thee, and show thee great and mighty things, which thou knowest not (Jeremiah 33:3).

I am the vine, ye are the branches: He that abideth in me, and I in him, the same bringeth forth much fruit: for without me ye can do nothing (John 15:5).

And he spake a parable unto them to this end, that men ought always to pray, and not to faint (Luke 18:1).

The pulpit committee must consider the candidate's sermon as one of the determining factors in the process of electing a pastor.

The pulpit committee may inquire with another believer or association for recommendation of other candidates. The pulpit committee with the consent of the congregation may visit a church to consider another pastor to be a candidate for the church. The pulpit committee can observe the pastor, his sermon, and his pulpit ethics and give a report for recommendation.

Organizing the Pulpit Committee
Purpose: John 15:5

1. When a Baptist Church is without a pastor, leadership falls to its Board of Deacons, or to a "Joint-Board" composed of Board of Deacons and Trustees.

There are at least three functions of the Board or pulpit committee.

    a) Supply pulpit with preachers
    b) Arrange care for the sick, funerals, communion
    c) Nurture and care for the church's spiritual life

2. Pulpit committee calls special meetings of the congregation to deal with problems that may arise.

3. The number of persons in the pulpit committee may vary, depending on the size of the congregation.

4. Pulpit committee must follow through with the candidate by phone call or letter to give him an appointment to preach.

5. Committee decides on what candidate to pursue.

6. Committee arranges interview with candidate.

7. If committee is not satisfied with all of the candidates, go back to step number one.

The Scripture says,

> teaching them to observe all things whatsoever I have commanded you: and lo, I am with you always, even unto the end of the world (Matt. 28:20). Amen.

A well-trained candidate can be the life of the church as he seeks God's guidance and direction to train those under his watch. According to Scriptures, train up a child in the way he should go and when he is old, he will not depart from it (Proverbs 22:6).

Interviewing the Candidate

The interview should be held in a meeting room where there is privacy and a good setting for a formal discussion. The meeting should be within a timely manner and revolve around the candidate's resume or application for further clarification and understanding.

The interview may consist of a series of concerns, such as what is the candidate's family or marital status, what are his visions, goals, and ideas for the growth of the church.

The committee is not to make any promises or commitment to the candidate. Thank the candidate for his interest in the church. The committee may discuss briefly about what kind of salary is expected.

The committee has three possible decisions following the interviews with all of the candidates.

> 1) The committee can seek further information about the candidate and delay its decision until a later date.
>
> 2) The committee can present him to the congregation for election.
>
> 3) The committee and the congregation can move to the next name on the list of applications.

If and when the committee has made a final decision and makes a recommendation to the congregation, then the congregation accepts and agrees on the committee's recommendation, and finally the congregation votes on the candidate.

Then, a deacon, trustee, or a representative of the church who was present at the meeting would contact the newly elected pastor to inform him of the church's decision, to ask him if he will accept the position of the church, and to let him know what salary is offered.

HOW TO CALL A PASTOR: CHANGE-CHAIN

The church that is vacant must consider your ways. Most churches have a problem with change. A newly elected pastor who has no training by the Holy Spirit will make the mistake of trying to make changes too soon, which may create friction, chaos, and problems. Ultimately, the newly elected pastor may lose the church.

However, there are some people in the church who want change and others who do not want change. It is best for both the pastor and congregation to agree to let it alone and pray and visit the Scriptures to make the necessary changes.

It is never a good thing to fight the spiritual leader; both the pulpit and pew must spend time in prayer together and allow the Holy Spirit to be in control of the Church. The Church belongs to Jesus Christ. The life of the Church is prayer and the doctrine of Jesus Christ in the life of the believer.

The newly elected pastor is going to make some changes, but he must have the wisdom of God on which changes to make. There are some brush fires that will be put out by themselves if you leave them alone. We must be patient with ourselves and the church.

There are some traditions that need to be kept and some that need to be deleted. For example, there are no biblical annual days in the Bible.

The problem all church people is that they think the Church belongs to them. There are only two groups of people that think the church belongs to them and those are the pastor and the church members.

There is a book in my library that asks, "why do churches die?" One of the answers is "tradition."

Sometimes, the pew gives evidence that he or she has never been born-again by the fruit he or she bears.

*The Church needs to pray the Word of God through faith and petition to God to send an undershepherd who is humble and Holy Spirit-led and fed. The Church also needs to humble itself, repent, confess their sins, and turn from their wicked ways. When the Church is in conflict, it is a combination of both an untrained pulpit and an untrained pew.

The church may have had a former pastor with a tenure of 30 to 40 years. Yet, an untrained, newly elected pastor can tear down what the former pastor built.

The best person to train the pulpit and the pew is the Holy Spirit; you must stay in his presence and spend time with him.

When a church has a pastor with a tenure of 30 to 40 years pass away or retire, it is difficult to make an adjustment to a new pastor. There is not another one like the former pastor.

The problem we have in our churches is the traditional mindset of the pastor as the only one who is supposed to tend to the spiritual things of the church, and the deacon handles the money. This mindset is not biblical.

According to Acts 4:34-35,

> Neither was there any among them that lacked: for as many as were possessors of lands or houses sold them, and brought the prices of the things that were sold, And laid them down at the apostles' feet: and distribution was made unto every man according as he had need.

The problem in the Church is described in the book, *Release of the Spirit,* by Watchman Nee. Watchman Nee said in his book that we are spirit, soul, and body. He also said that when we are born-again, our spirit-man is born-again, and the born-again spirit releases himself into the soulish realm and saves us. Sometimes, we can harden our hearts to our soulish realm.

The Scripture says in Hebrews 3,

---

* Run on

Wherefore (as the Holy Ghost saith, To day if ye will hear his voice, Harden not your hearts, as in the provocation, in the day of temptation in the wilderness (v. 7-8).

Take heed, brethren, lest there be in any of you an evil heart of unbelief, in departing from the living God (v. 12).

While it is said, To day if ye will hear his voice, harden not your hearts, as in the Provocation (v. 15).

*The Body of Christ includes some people who are not intimate with God nor intelligent and who display ungodly behavior and conduct in the presence of God. These people may not be believers of Jesus Christ, nor Holy-Spirit-led. The Scripture says in Matthew 5:16, "Let you light so shine before men, that they see your good works, and glorify your Father which is in heaven."

In most cases, it is a family church where the children do not have the courage to sit their mothers and fathers down when they are fighting their spiritual leader, the pastor,

The born-again spirit has a difficult time trying to release himself into the soulish realm. The soulish realm is our intellect, will, and emotion. The Holy Spirit has a hard time trying to get us to submit to his will.

Psalm 37:23 says, "the steps of a good man is ordered by the Lord; and he delighted in his way."

The Lord has never ordered the steps of a good man to portray ungodly conduct in the Body of Christ. This Scripture sounds good, but many people do not practice it and that is the reason many of our homes, churches, and communities are in the condition they are in.

There are some people, as well as the pastor, who let their titles lead them into pride.

The Lord spoke to me and said, your eternal security is not in the pulpit, only in Jesus Christ. There is not eternal security in a title, and many people get offended when you do

---

* Run on sentences

not address them as Reverend, Pastor, Bishop, Evangelist, etc. There are over 13 titles in the Bible and all could be lost.

If there is no change in a person's attitude, behavior, and conduct when the newly elected pastor becomes the overseer, this will cause conflicts between the pulpit and the pew.

One of the greatest problems in many of the Black Baptist churches is among the pastor and the Deacon Board, which are the only two biblical offices in the church.

> Paul said, "therefore if any man be in Christ, he is a new creature: old things are passes; behold, all things are become new" (2 Corinthians 5:17).

How to Call a Pastor:
How to Deal with Burnouts

When calling a pastor to serve as the undershepherd, sometimes we can very easily become burnt-out. What contributes to burnouts? It can be a combination of things.

When you begin to experience feelings of burnout, you must acknowledge those feelings to discover what is causing it and how to prevent it from recurring. Burnouts can be related to stress, depression, frustration, disappointment, anxieties, low self-esteem, and unfulfilled assignments, dreams, goals, and visions.

We fail to recognize the stress of our daily routine and workload and try to do everything on our own, and then we are left feeling burnt-out. Burnouts can be family related, job related, church related, and even community participation related. Sometimes others can recognize burnout in you sooner than you can.

The way to deal with burnouts is to acknowledge them and find balance. We must take frequent breaks, acknowledge that we need some help, and then go get help.

Sometimes people can burnout in church from carrying the workload of three or four positions they feel nobody else can do but them. Sometimes others refuse to carry the load, and oftentimes we do not have quality leaders nor trained leaders in the pulpit and the pew.

Burnouts can be caused when others depend on us for everything, and we do not have the courage to say no. We must pray a prayer,

> Then saith he [Jesus] unto his disciples, The harvest truly is plenteous, but the labourers are few; Pray ye therefore the Lord of the harvest, that he will send forth labourers into his harvest (Matthew 9:37-38).

What can cause burnouts within the Body of Christ? Traditions have caused some burnouts. We spend too much time at church and not enough time at home and not enough time with God. Pastors and leaders can engage in too many church activities until they cannot hear the voice of God; our intimacy with God can become dull. Trying to fulfill two or more positions in the church can cause our spirit, soul, and body to become weary and weak toward hearing and knowing the voice of God.

Some of the things that can make you neglect time spent with God include working two or more jobs, paying bills, cooking, trying to do house chores, trying to deal with two or more children, working hours of overtime, trying to make ends meet, and trying to be a caregiver to the sick and going in and out of doctor offices and the hospital.

There are Scriptures that give us examples of how to deal with burnouts and how to prevent burnouts. In the book of Numbers 11,

> And when the people complained, it displeased the Lord: and the Lord heard it; and his anger was kindled; and the fire of the Lord burnt among them, and consumed them that were in the uttermost parts of the camp. And the people cried unto Moses; and when Moses prayed unto the Lord, the fire was quenched (v. 1-2).

> Then Moses heard the people weep throughout their families, every man in the door of his tent: and the anger of the Lord was kindled greatly; Moses also was displeased (v. 10). [See Numbers 11:1-35]

Moses confesses,

> I am not able to bear all this people alone, because it is too heavy for me (Numbers 11:14).

God gives Moses some help,

> And the Lord said unto Moses, Gather unto me seventy men of the elders of Israel, whom thou knowest to be the elders of the people, and officers over them; and bring them unto the tabernacle of the congregation, that they may stand there with thee. And I will come down and talk with thee there: and I will take of the spirit which is upon thee, and will put it upon them; and they shall bear the burden of the people with thee, that thou bear it not thyself alone (Numbers 11:16-17).

Moses was dealing with the children of Israel by judging their concerns when his father-in-law advised him to get some able men to help him.

> And it came to pass on the morrow, that Moses sat to judge the people: and the people stood by Moses from the morning unto the evening. And when Moses' father in law saw all that he did to the people, he said, What is this thing that thou doest to the people? why sittest thou thyself alone, and all the people stand by thee from morning unto even? And Moses said unto his father in law, Because the people come unto me to enquire of God: When they have a matter, they come unto me; and I judge between one and another, and I do make them know the statutes of God, and his laws. And Moses' father in law said unto him, The thing that thou doest is not good. Thou wilt surely wear away, both thou, and this people that is with thee: for this thing is too heavy for thee; thou art not able to perform it thyself alone (Exodus 18:13-18).

In order to prevent burnouts, we must follow the leadership style Jesus Christ used when he chose his leadership team.

> And he goeth up into a mountain, and calleth unto him whom he would: and they came unto him. And he ordained twelve, that they should be with him, and that he might send them forth to preach, And to have power to heal sicknesses, and to cast out devils (Mark 3:13-15).

After these things the Lord appointed other seventy also, and sent them two and two before his face into every city and place, whither he himself would come (Luke 10:1).

We also have another example in Scripture to prevent burnouts when the twelve apostles had the multitudes choose seven men to take care of the Grecians, who were neglected from daily administration, while they give themselves to prayer and the Word of God [See Acts 6:1-7].

The way we can handle burnouts is also described in Galatians 6:2,

Bear ye one another's burdens, and so fulfil the law of Christ.

Burnouts can be resolved if we,

Let no corrupt communication proceed out of your mouth, but that which is good to the use of edifying, that it may minister grace unto the hearers. And grieve not the holy Spirit of God, whereby ye are sealed unto the day of redemption. Let all bitterness, and wrath, and anger, and clamour, and evil speaking, be put away from you, with all malice: And be ye kind one to another, tenderhearted, forgiving one another, even as God for Christ's sake hath forgiven you (Ephesians 4:29-32).

HOW TO CALL A PASTOR: CHURCH SPLITS

Churches may split if they do not have proper training and teaching in church leadership and Christian leadership. There is a difference between church leadership and Christian leadership.

People can train and teach church leadership. However, the Holy Spirit is the only one who can train and teach Christian leadership, which only can happen when both the pulpit and pew are converted and spend time with the Holy Spirit.

> But the Comforter, which is the Holy Ghost, whom the Father will send in my name, he shall teach you all things, and bring all things to your remembrance, whatsoever I have said unto you (John 14:26).

There are many people in the Baptist Church who know very little of the person of the Holy Spirit. Churches split because of the mindset of people. Some people think they own the church, some think they can hire and fire the pastor, some think the money belongs to them, some have a traditional mindset and refuse to change.

Some people have clichés in the church, and some feel like they control the whole church; we call them "bell-cow." Churches split sometimes because the pulpit is sleeping with the pew. This type of behavior and conduct gives evidence that this person is not saved,

> for the tree is known by his fruit" (Matthew 12:33).

The Scripture says,

> God is not the author of confusion, but of peace, as in all churches of the saints (1 Corinthians 14:33).

God is a God of order. The Scripture says,

> Let all things be done decently and in order (1 Corinthians 14:40).

The Word of God teaches us in Matthew 5:9,

> Blessed are the peacemakers; for they shall be called the children of God.

Church splits are caused by the ones who are not governed by the Holy Spirit. People in leadership may have more influence over some people than the Holy Spirit does. Churches split because of lack of teaching from both the pulpit and the pew. There is no hunger and thirst for God's righteousness.

> Blessed are they which do hunger and thirst after righteousness: for they shall be filled (Matthew 5:6).

The Body of Christ at large does not support Sunday School, Bible Study, and does not pay tithes. The pastors also have a difficult time getting people to support prayer ministry. Scripture says,

> Not forsaking the assembling of ourselves together, as the manner of some is; but exhorting one another: and so much the more, as ye see the day approaching (Hebrews 10:25).

It is both the pastors and the members who blame the pastor for the split. It is a combination of an untrained pulpit and an untrained pew, both who have not totally submitted themselves under the authority and power of the Holy Spirit.

There is a passage of Scripture that says,

> Woe be unto the pastors that destroy and scatter the sheep of my pasture! saith the Lord (Jeremiah 23:1).

Sometimes churches may not split because of the pastor's preaching and teaching ability but because of his leadership ability.

The flock scatters sometimes from a lack of obedience and submissiveness to the pastor.

Obey them that have the rule over you, and submit yourselves: for they watch for your souls, as they that must give account, that they may do it with joy, and not with grief: for that is unprofitable for you (Hebrew 13:17).

Take heed therefore unto yourselves, and to all the flock, over the which the Holy Ghost hath made you overseers, to feed the church of God, which he hath purchased with his own blood (Acts 20:28).

Paul said in 1 Corinthians 1:10,

Now I beseech you, brethren, by the name of our Lord Jesus Christ, that ye all speak the same thing, and that there be no divisions among you; but that ye be perfectly joined together in the same mind and in the same judgment.

The Holy Spirit has to be the common denominator that keeps the church together through the Word of God. The average pulpit and pew very seldom search the Scriptures to resolve issues in the church.

We seek other resources, opinions, and advice. We also seek answers to our problems regarding how we think and how we feel on the internet, Facebook, Twitter, websites, and Instagram.

Paul said to the Philippian Church,

Fulfil ye my joy, that ye be likeminded, having the same love, being of one accord, of one mind. Let nothing be done through strife or vainglory; but in lowliness of mind let each esteem other better than themselves. Look not every man on his own things, but every man also on the things of others. Let this mind be in you, which was also in Christ Jesus: (Philippians 2:2-5).

The church splits because of problems the newly elected pastor inherited and problems he created by making unnecessary changes.

There was a situation at a church where the newly elected pastor wanted to remove some shrubs around the church, and the deacon wanted the shrubs to remain around the church because they had been there for over fifteen years. This issue caused a problem between the newly elected pastor and the deacon.

There is no eternal security in any shrubs. The deacon's mindset was the pastor only should be concerned about the spiritual things in the church. The deacon should be concerned about the building, grounds, and property. This is a traditional mindset of church leadership. The biblical deacons are referred to as men in Acts 6:1-6; they did not fight or argue with the twelve apostles.

As a result, the newly elected pastor lost a faithful member of the church. It is not worth a pastor or member leaving or losing the church over some mess like that. That is an example of an untrained pulpit and an untrained pew; sometimes the pulpit can force his will upon the pew.

> Neither as being lords over God's heritage, but being examples to the flock (1 Peter 5:3).

This matter should have been left alone. It is one of those brush fires that we leave alone and trust God to handle.

All churches regardless of denomination, race, creed, or color is a revolving door. There is a difference between the Church and the congregation.

The Church consists of born-again, redeemed, regenerated, converted, transformed, saved, sanctified, and spirit-filled individuals. Church comes from the Greek word *Ekklesia*, which means called out one, called out of the world, yet in the world. See John 17:6, 9, 11-19. The congregation are people who join the church, put their name on the roll, and are baptized in the name of the Father, Son, and Holy Ghost, yet never give their life to Christ and never work out their own salvation.

> Work out your own salvation with fear and trembling (Philippians 2:12).

It is important that we, the Body of Christ, embrace sound doctrine so that we may have a healthy church. A healthy church is a strong church—strong in their theology and strong in their relationship with the Savior. A healthy church gives birth to healthy members.

Sometimes churches split because the pulpit and the pew are weak in their doctrine and very easily influenced by others in the church, follow the crowd, and later return to their former church.

The Holy Spirit does not split churches. Peter and the other apostles answered and said,

> We ought to obey God rather than men (Acts 5:29).

> And now I say unto you, Refrain from these men, and let them alone: for if this counsel or this work be of men, it will come to nought: But if it be of God, ye cannot overthrow it; lest haply ye be found even to fight against God (Acts 5:38-39).

Sometimes, some churches do not survive splits because the pew was influenced by the pastor, rather than the leading of the Holy Spirit. Later, the pulpit and pew may experience feelings of guilt from the decisions made.

Some churches split for the wrong motives or reasons. The pastor or pulpit organize what they call, "their own church." For example, the pastor or pew can live whatever lifestyle they want without being dismissed from the church; that is not God's Church. God is not obligated to bless or add to that kind of mindset.

Then, there are those who are genuine with good and right motives who organize in order to have peace among themselves.

> But God hath called us to peace (1 Corinthians 7:15).

> Blessed are the peacemakers; they shall be called the children of God (Matthew 5:9).

God loves all people and will sometimes wait a while for that split church to see and recognize their sins, their faults, and problems so that they will confess and repent of their behaviors and be healed of their conduct and character. The Holy Spirit will make a divine assignment to that church, to be ministered and to be saved.

> Who will have all men to be saved, and to come to unto the knowledge of truth (1 Timothy 2:4).

The church of today must pursue becoming a healthy church that will give birth to healthy, kingdom-minded disciples of Jesus Christ.

There have been churches that survive the split because God never told them, the pastors or the people, to organize. God is not obligated to bless a ministry he did not speak into the heart of an individual. God the Father, God the Son, and God the Holy Spirit in many instances is not orchestrating many of the man-made ministries.

There have been pastors and members that feel bad and guilty about the moves they have made. If it is not of the Holy Spirit, He will convict you of your decisions, and sometimes He will not let you prosper. If the visions, ideas, and dreams are not of God, that ministry is going to soon crumble and crash and turn to trash.

It is very important for the newly elected pulpit and pew to be trained by the Holy Spirit and to use wisdom and good judgement to make changes, rebuild the ministry, and repair the damage that has been done. Now the newly elected pulpit (pastor) has to look through the rubble to find him some qualified leaders to move the church forward.

Churches must have a sound biblical structure, or it will be just a matter of time before there is another split. It is important to provide some type of leadership training to the untrained pulpit and untrained pew once a week, once a month, or once every three months

> Train up a child in the way he should go: and when he is old, he will not depart from it (Proverbs 22:6).

When there is leadership training available in our city and in our region, other pastors and members do not attend or support it because it is not at their church. Everybody is a leader and should seek leadership training and skills to help develop their character, conduct, pulpit ethics, and church membership doctrine. There are some pastors who do not want other pastors and laymen to teach or train their congregation, God's sheep.

When a church splits, other churches feel like they are growing when they receive members from another church. Those churches are receiving transfers, rather than new converts.

Some members who leave with the new pastor's church split may be ashamed to go back to their home church. The church's split can cause bitterness, resentment, hostility, and anger between some of the members of the new church split and the other church. Both the pastor and members may experience unforgiveness toward one another.

> Let all bitterness, and wrath, and anger, and clamour, and evil speaking, be put away from you, with all malice: And be ye kind one another, tenderhearted, forgiving one another, even as God for Christ's sake hath forgiven you (Ephesians 4:31-32).

When a church splits or becomes vacant, those who are left from the pew or members may have the perspective that they are doing good. However, from God's perspective, they are not doing good without a shepherd or an undershepherd for the scattered people.

> And they were scattered, because there is no shepherd: and they became meat to all the beasts of the field, when they were scattered (Ezekiel 34:5).

Many who fight against spiritual leaders (pastors) fail to realize that God will forgive you, but he will deal with you later. Sometimes, the entire church has to suffer being disciplined, and the purpose of the discipline is to correct a person's or the church's behavior, attitude, thoughts, and conduct.

> If ye endure chastening, God dealeth with you as with sons; for what son is he whom the father chastened not? But if ye be without chastisement, where of all are partakers, then are ye bastards, and not sons (Hebrews 12:7-8).

> Touch not my anointed, and do my prophet no harm (Psalm 105:15).

When a church becomes vacant,

> God himself find a man that execute judgement, that seeketh the truth (Jeremiah 5:1).

> God would also seek for a man to make up the hedge and stand in the gap, but he found none (Ezekiel 22:30).

It is very clear why we have problems with leadership in the church, primarily because of carnal-minded members who are divided over issues, traditions, annual days, and membership. Also, sometimes, the pastor can make it seem like the Church is their own instead of Jesus Christ's.

According to the Webster Dictionary, "purpose" means aim, intention, mission, desire, expectation, intent.

God never desires or has intentions of his Church splitting or for the confusion that is happening in our societies. The Church was established for God's purpose, and God's intentions and expectations were for the Church to be operated by the divine direction and guidance of the Holy Spirit.

The Church must be trained and taught, as well as equipped to understand the purpose of the Trinity and to know their function in the Body of Christ. The Church also must be trained and informed on the purpose of the biblical functions of the five gifts given to the Body of Christ in order to prevent ongoing divisions in the Church.

God's purpose and mission of the church is recorded in Matthew 28:19-20.

> God's plan and purpose for his Son is to provide mankind with salvation
> which gives us Eternal security, by giving us eternal life (John 6:68).

God's plan and purpose for the Holy Spirit is to keep us, guide us, comfort us, and seal us unto the Day of Redemption [See John 14:26 and Ephesians 1:13]. God's will was never for his Church to split or to divide. This is the work of Satan, working through the minds and hearts of the members.

> The thief cometh not, but for to steal, and to kill, and to destroy: I am come
> that they may might have life, and that they might have it more abundantly
> (John 10:10).

Sometimes, we can forget who the Church belongs to and try to have church without Jesus Christ and the power of the Holy Spirit.

Jesus said, without me ye can do nothing (John 15:5).

The Church and her mission has become powerless and has lost her influence in the Body of Christ because of the lack of prayer and unity in the homes, churches, and communities. Jesus Christ came to reconcile man and the universe back to fellowship and relationship with God, which the first Adam lost and the second Adam came to restore.

THE PROCESS OF CALLING A PASTOR TO A VACANT CHURCH/PULPIT GOD'S WAY

ISAIAH 55:8-9

JESUS TRAINED THE TWELVE FOR 3 1/2 YRS.

THE LEADERSHIP STYLE OF JESUS

HOW TO MAKE A LASTING IMPACT

WHERE LEADERS COME FROM?

This idea of the leadership style of Jesus, is a book, by Michael Youssef, deals with the question in his book, Why did Jesus choose the Twelve. Many churches are looking for leaders in the wrong places, The Holy Spirit has not lead a church to advertise in the newspaper, dvd, social media, for a pastor, to fill the Lord's pulpit. The church is Jesus Christ, then we must trust Him through much prayer and supplication to make the divine assigment. The scriptures teach us." For they being ignorant of God's righteousness, and going about to established their own righteousness, and have not submitted themselves unto righteousness of God Ro. 10:3". The church wants to play "short-cuts" with God, instead of committing themselves to unified scriptural prayers, "lean not toward our own understanding Pr. 3:5". There is no leadership training for the associate ministers to prepare them for pastorial, the associate ministers do not seek seminary training, or any type of education to give God something to work with. God is looking for leaders according to Jeremiah 5:1 Run to and fro through the streets of Jerusalem, and see now, and know, and seek in the broad places thereof, if ye can find a man, if there be any that executeth judgment, that seeketh the truth: and I will pardon it. Also God, speaks, to Ezekiel 22:30 And I sought for a man among them to make up the hedge, and stand in the gap before me for the land, that I should not destroy it: but I found none.

There is not a school or university that can teach a preacher how to pastor. Only his experiences and relationship with God and the peoples will train him how to pastor. It is very questionable, why, pastors, do not have any trained, potential associates, he can recommend to a vacant church, that can filled the gap, so that God's sheep won't scatter. The pulpit is the most sacred place in church. The church ought to be a place of refuge, spiritual healing, love, joy, peace, and a good worshipping experience.

To make a lasting impact in leadership one must remain in the presence of the Holy Spirit, to receive meditations, revelations, and, illuminations, to give proper intepretations. I feel the Holy Spirit has no need of assigning two or three churches to one person/pastor, when the scriptures teaches us, "No man can served two masters: for either he will hate the one, and love the other: or else he will hold to the one; and despise the other. Ye cannot serve God and mammon. (money)." The pastor must train and teach the body of Christ, biblical principles how God uses the tithes and offerings to take care the priests, and his family, in the Old Testament. Num. 18:9-19. All the best of the oil, and all the best of the wine, and the wheat, and the "firstfruits" of them which they offer unto the Lord, them have I given thee. v. 12. The church must bless the pastor with the very best. The Holy Spirit has not Influenced one pastor to pastor two churches, this can be a form of greed. (stronghold of income). This is not good structure for the church, or the pastor. "And Moses father in law said unto him, The thing that thou doest is not good." Ex. 18:17. "...muzzle not the ox that treadeth out the corn. 1 Cor. 9:9," If we have sown unto you spiritual things, is it a great thing if we reap your carnal things? 1 Cor. 9:11". "Let the elders that rule well be counted worthy of double honor, especially they who labour in the word and doctrine. 1 Tim. 5:17".

Many of our African American, non bi-vocational pastors are full-time, yet, do not have full benefits from the church they served, because the church/deacons is controlling the money. The church loves the idea of having a healthy bank account and the pastor has been there over 20 years with no health insurance, no retirement, no life insurance, the pastor is living on his wife job benefits, because the church rather have a good healthy

GOD'S DIVINE ALIGNMENT / GOD'S DIVINE ASSIGNMENT   147

bank account, and the pastor takes a risk every day with and without health insurance. It is the church's responsibility to take care of "their pastor". The pastor is the "only" paid position in the Bible. Some pastors right now desire to step down, because of burnout, poor health, no visions, no goals, no zeal to go any further, the untrained pulpit need somebody to pull him out the "PIT." HE HAS BEEN ROASTED AND BARBEQUED, by the untrained pew. "1 kings 19:4 It is enough: now, O Lord, take away my life; for I am not better than my fathers". What do, you do, when you don't know what to do? Pray. The pastors and the churches ought to be ashamed of themselves to allow this type of "sin" to be tolerated. Headz Up, Jesus Is Coming Soon.

The process of finding a pastor is sometimes difficult, and sometimes it is hard to keep a pastor because of poor quality structure benefits, and poor quality structure of trained leadership teams. It is hard to pastor a church and work a job too. Pastoring is a risky business especially when you got a untrained congregation who refuses to take "good" care of their pastor. Every pastor ought to be treated with dignity and respect, and honor. "And we beseech you brethren to know them which labour among you, and are over you in the Lord, and admonished you; And to esteem them very highly in love for their works sake. And be at peace among yourselves. 1 Thess. 5:12-13

The Holy Spirit does not have the impact on the body of Christ today as the New Testament church. And when the day of Pentecost was fully come, they were all with one accord in one place. Acts 2:1. The process of calling a pastor to a vacant church must be done God's way, the church and the pastor will benefit from this type structure as he labours in the Word and doctrine. This is not too hard for God...and there is nothing to hard for thee Jer. 32:17.

Pray   Stay   Lay   PAY

1. Pray. The pastor and church ought to set aside a weekly prayer meeting together to strenghtened the church family... but as for me and my house, we will serve the Lord. Josh. 24:15. ...he kneeled upon his knees three times a day, and prayed, and gave thanks before God, as he did aforetime. Dan. 6:10. Create in me a clean heart, O God: and renew a right spirit within me. Psa. 51:10. These and many more prayers to pray as we encounter every day life. Be ye not therefore like unto them: for your Father knoweth what things ye have need of before ye ask him. Matt. 6:8. ...And when he had sent the

multitudes away, he went up into a mountain apart to pray; and when the evening was come, he was alone. Matt. 14:23, My God, my God why hast thou forsaken me. Matt. 27:46. Jesus had moments with the Father. And in the morning, rising up a great while before day, he went out, and departed into a solitary place, and there prayed. Mk. 1:35. And there was one Ana, a prophetess, the daughter of Phanuel, of the tribe of Aser: she was of a great age, and had lived with an husband seven years from her virginity; And she was a widow of about fourscore and four years, which departed not from the temple, but served God with fastings and prayers night and day Lk. 2:36-37. ...that men ought always to pray. Lk. 18:1.

2. Stay. When the pastor and the church pray together they stay together, And when he had considered the thing, he came to the house of Mary the mother of John, who surname was Mark; where many gathered together praying. Ac. 12:12. A trained pulpit/pastor and trained pew will encourage members to stay. Behold, how good and how pleasant it for brethren to dwell together in unity! Psa. 133:1. For the body is not one member, but many. 1 Cor. 12:14. Real, genuine, authentic, true, honest-to-goodness, praise and worship will make people want to stay. Heartfelt, good hospitality, and fellowship, and warm welcome make people look forward to coming again. "I was glad when they said unto me, Let us go into the house of the Lord. Psa. 122:1.

3. Lay. We must lay ourselves prostrate, and surrender, the total man, to our Lord and Saviour Jesus Christ. We must lay aside every weight, and the sin which so easily beset us, and let us run with patience the race that is set before us. Heb. 12:1. Wherefore laying aside all malice (ill-feeling), and all guile (dishonesty), and hypocrisies (lip service), and envies (grudge), and all evil speaking. 1 Pt. 2:1. Confess your faults one to another, and pray one for another, that ye may be healed. The effectual fervent prayer of a righteous man availeth much. Jas. 5:16. In the process of calling a pastor the church must lay aside all differences, prior to the newly elected candidate arrival as pastor. There must be a good relationship between the deacon ministry, and the pastor, in order, for it to be a healthy church. We must follow the leadership style Jesus, He and his disciples, didn't cross words, and the model church, the twelve apostles, and the seven men, didn't cross words or argue with one another. Become a biblical deacon, instead, of a tradition deacon. REPENT.

4. Pay. There must be a conviction of the church, pay tithes and offerings in worship, to finance God's kingdom. Some only pay their tithes and not their offerings, Malachi 3:8-10

says, Will a man robbed God? Yet ye have robbed thee? In tithes and offerings. Some think the tithes came under the law, actually, the tithes begain before the law. Melchizedek, gave tithes to Abraham." And Melchizedek king of Salem brought forth bread and wine: and he was the priest of the most high God. And he blessed him, and said, Blessed be Abram of the most high God, possessor of heaven and earth: And blessed be the most high God, which hath delivered thine enemies into thy hand. And he gave him tithes of all. Gen. 14:18-20

Pay. "For I have not shunned (concealed, kept away from, taken advantage of) to declare unto you all the counsel of God. (guidance, information). We must understand not tithing will not send you to hell or heaven, there is no eternal life in tithing. The only way a person will not receive eternal life is to reject Jesus Christ as their Saviour. The purpose of the tithes and offering. 1. Church to Provide for The Pastor and his Family. 2. To Experience A Blessed Life. 3. To Finance God' kingdom. 4. Maintenance of Church Property. 5. Outreach Ministry. There has been some people who get upset at the pastor and church and stop paying their tithes and offerings. They're not hurting anyone but themselves. It's God's money they're withholding, God will eventually, deal with them. YE ARE CURSED WITH A CURSE. Mal. 3:9. You're going to pay, dearly. Be a grace giver, Give, and it shall be given unto you: good measure, pressed down, and shaken together, and running over, shall men give into your bosom. For with the same measure that ye mete withal it shall be measured to you again. Lk. 6:38

Pay. The question has been asked is the word "tithes" in the New Testament? Yes. references:

* Mt. 23:23 * Lk. 18:12 * Heb. 7:1-9 Tithing is a "TEST" of your faith. ...It is more blessed to give than to receive. Ac. 20:35.

Pastors Leadership Prayer

O Lord I am thankful and grateful for your divine alignment for your divine assignment. Thank you for all my trials, tribulations (Jn. 16:33). O Lord I must continue remind myself you are the owner and operator of the church and she cannot function without you (Jn. 15:5) O Lord help me allow the Holy Spirit trained me be the administrator and overseer of your heritage being example to the flock. According to scriptures the term CEO Chief Executive Officer is not what the Holy Spirit mention in scriptures:

Take heed therefore unto yourselves, and to all the flock, over which the Holy Ghost hath made you overseers (not CEO'S) to feed the church (WORD) of God, which he had purchased with his own (BLOOD) (Acts 20:28). O Lord help me trained men/deacons to know their duties and responsibilities from a biblcal perspective.

I am experiencing afflictions (1 Thess. 3:3) and struggle with the Archenemy (satan) Father God many despiseth, despiseth not man, but God, who hath also given unto us his holy Spirit (1 Thess. 3:8). Father God you has allowed this your servant to be put in trust with the gospel, even so we speak: not as pleasing men, but God, which trieth (test) our hearts (1 Thess. 2:4). O Lord give this your servant guidance and direction to lead your sheeps (Pr. 3:5-6). O Lord help me to be a motivator leader motivating your people to paritcipate and co-operate and take an interest and support every function of the church.

O Lord you said, He that heareth you hearth me: and he that despiseth you despiseth me: and he hath despiseth me despiseth him that sent me (Lk. 9:16). O Lord you said...the harvest is truly is plenteous, but the labours are few: Pray ye therefore the Lord of the harvest, that he will send forth labours into his harvest (Matt. 9:37-38).

Heavenly Father bless me with visions and goals to accomplished the divine assignment. Father I pray we all be ready when Jesus come (Jn. 14:1-4).

O Lord I have a desire to continue this assignment or accept another one according to your will. O Lord, in spite what problems we have had: I will bless the Lord at all times: his praise shall continue be in my mouth. My soul shall make her boast in the Lord: the humble shall hear thereof, and be glad. O magnify the Lord with me, and let us exalt his name together. O taste and see that the Lord is good: blessed is the man that trusted in him (Psa. 34:1,2,3,8).

O Lord I believe things are going to get better: For his anger endureth but a moment: in his favor is life: weeping may endure for, but joy cometh in the morning (Psa. 30:5). O Lord I pray these souls have eternal life: And this is life eternal, that they might know thee the only true God, and Jesus Christ whom thou has sent (Jn. 17:3).

Heavenly Father: I pray that you bless me to be faithful over those you has given me the ability to served: His lord said unto him, Well done, thou good and faithful servant: thou has been faithful over a few things, I will make thee ruler over many things: enter thou into the joy of thy lord (Matt. 25:21).

Father God thank you for many souls you saved under my watch: Likewise, I say unto you, there is joy in the presence of God over one sinner that repenteth (Lk. 15:10). In the name of Jesus Christ. Amen.

BEWARE OF POTHOLED

MENTALITY/INTELLECT

IN THE PUPLIT/PEW

Pot is a container, vessel, kettle, pan, jug, jar, bucket, cup, can, pitcher, mug, bowl.

Potable is fit for drinking, uncontaminated, drinkable, clean, upolluted, fresh, pure, sanitary.

As a school bus aide to the school bus driver in the school system one morning after dropping the students off at school on our way to returned to the bus stop. The bus driver made a right turn at the red light and run overa pothole more than one and the potholes was very wide and deep that it cause the bus to tilt as we was traveling it even cause the driver to complained about it. When I came home I called the city street department to report the potholes for repair it was obvious and noticeable to those of us riding the bus.

But we have this treasure in earthen vessels, that the excellency of the power may be of God, and not in us (2 Cor. 4:7). When the head is messed up the body can't function. ...the whole head is sick, and the whole heart faint (burnout, give up, quit) (Isa. 1:5) Sometimes potholes can be dangerous and painful to your vehicles possibility of damage your tires and rims. To correct the potholes from any problems in the future it must be filled with tar. Well, sometimes a vacant congregation/pulpit as well as a pulpit already filled can be a pothole when the preacher/pastor does not spend quality time in prayer (Acts 6:4). A pothole is a void or empty like a pitcher, or cup, sometimes contaminated with debris, water, dirt, etc.

This can be the same way in a spiritual matter when only the Holy Spirit can filled the emptiness of the pulpit's heart, hand, and head. Brethren my heart's desire and prayer to God for Israel is, that they might be saved (Ro. 10:1). Draw nigh to God, and he will draw nigh to you. Cleanse your hands, ye sinners: and purify your hearts, ye double minded (Jas. 4:8). And he is the dead of the body (...Col. 1:18). Congregations can experience many potholes for candidates for pastor. For this people is waxed gross, and their are dull of hearing, and their eyes they have closed; least at any time they see with their eyes, and hear with their ears, and should understand with their heart, and should be converted, and I shoul heal them. But blessed are your eyes, for they see: and your ears, for they hear (Matt. 13:15-16).

There is a emptiness in the pulpit of powerless and prayerlessness sermons who does not take the time to make adequate preparations in the WORD (John 1:1) to transform the pew (Ro. 12:1-3). The radio and T.V. ministry as well as countless short and lenghty conversations with local church members and pastors who is disgrumbled at one another. Neither the pastor or pew members spend hardly or very little time together in corporate prayers some churches experience AWHOL after Sunday's service and for prayer meeting and christian education training (Heb. 10:25).

A blind congregation can very easily elect a blind leader to lead them into some wide, deep, dirty, filthy, sewage, nastiness potholes.

But he answered and said, Every plant, which my heavenly Father hath not planted, shall be rooted up, Let them alone: they be blind leaders of the blind. If the blind lead the blind, both shall fall in the ditch (Matt. (15:13-14).

When the pulpit does not adequately sacrifice time and resources alone with quality meditation to equipped the body of Christ through Evangelism to equipped the world with knowledge and understanding (Jer. 3:15); (Matt. 28:18-20); (Eph. 4:11-16). This can hinder the growth of the church.

The members of the body of Christ filling potholes hearts/minds with excuses, overcommitment of work schedule, recreation activities, to tired for God and with other reasons for not fulfilling the Great Commission (Matt. 28:18-20).

Seek the Lord while he may be found, call ye upon him while he is near: for my thoughts are not your thoughts, neither are your ways my ways, saith the Lord. For as the heavens are higher than the earth, so are my ways higher than your ways, and my thoughts than your thoughts (Isa. 55:6, 8, 9). Michael Day's personal commentary is "My intelligence" is not your intelligence" v.8.

We must filled potholes with the intelligence of God (Phil. 2:5).

When tastes matter: O taste and see that the Lord is good: blessed is the man that trusted in him (Psa. 34:8).

I often hear people quote God is the head of my life but our hearts is crying out for worship only can be filled by the Holy Spirit.

...for the Father seeket such to worship him (John 4:23)

As newborn babes, desire the sincere milk of the word, that ye may grow thereby: If so be have tasted that the Lord is gracious (1 PT. 2:2-3).

THE DANGER OF A UNTRAINED

DEACON/ MEMBER

The danger of a untrained deacon or members of the church when they don't know their duties and resonsibilities they will neglect what they are assigned to do and become trouble-shooters and trouble-makers and burdened to the pastor rather than a blessing and help.

The deacons and members constantly nick-pick all the wrong doing of a pastor when the pastor has been unsuccessful to get these nick-pickers to come to Sunday School, Bible Class, and pay their tithes and offering.

I am a bus aide in the school system and I share with the driver how well they know their route and how well they know their students by their names. I sit behind the drivers somtimes trying to give them which directions to get to school much faster I tell all the drivers you go the way you know to go. (different drivers).

Pastors is the bus driver of the church with members sitting in the back seat trying to tell him how to pastor/drive the bus/church/ when a pastor know the route led by the Holy Spirit only the pastor knows the way, shows the way, and goes the way.

The steps of a good man are ordered by the Lord...(PS. 37:23).

In all thy ways acknowledge him, and he shall direct thy paths (Pr. 3:6)

O Lord, I know that the way of man is not in himself, it is not in man that walketh to direct his steps (Jer. 10:23).

WANT TO LEARN

The problem in leadership is dealing with leaders who don't want to learn but wants to be out front. Some pastors or churches don't have bible study because nobody attends this is not a healthy church when the leaders neglect the ministry of christian education.

And thou shalt teach them diligently unto thy children...(Deut. 6:7).

Take my yoke upon you: and learn of me...(Matt. 11:29).

But ye have not so learned Christ (Eph. 4:20).

And he said, How can I, except some man should guide me?...(Acts 8:31).

Not the forsaking the assembling of ourselves together...(Heb. 10:25).

Add on: Want to Learn, one must have a teachable spirit, trainable spirit, leaderable spirit, followable spirit, forgivable spirit, communiable, lovable spirit, savable spirit, humblable spirit, tithable spirit, giveable spirit, togetherable spirit (Psa. 133:1).

Resetting of the mind spirit (Phil. 2:5).

HOUSEHOLD

SALVATION

SCRIPTURE REFERENCES:

JOSHUA 6:22-23

MATTHEW 12:46-50

ACTS 10:1-8

ACTS 16:26-32

JOSHUA 24:15,7

JEREMIAH 8:11,14,15,20,21,22

JEREMIAH 9:1 THE WEEPING PROPHET

V.2 Treacherous—

Falsehearted, unfaithful, unreliable, misleading, untrustworthy, twofaced, insecure.

PRAYER

1. Scripturalize your prayer, Lord you said...Matt. 6:33

2. Spiritualize your prayer, Lord you said...John 4:24

3. Personalize your prayer, Lord you said...Jas. 1:22-23

1. ...that men ought always to pray and not to faint (give up). Lk. 18:1

2. ...but served God with fastings and prayers night and day. Lk. 2:37

3. ...he went out, and departed into a solitary (alone, lonely) place, and there prayed. Mk. 1:35.

4. ...in the morning will I direct my prayer unto thee, and will look up. Psa. 5:3

5. ...he kneeled upon his knees three times a day, and prayed, and gave thanks before his God, as he did aforetime. Daniel 6:10.

6. After this manner therefore pray ye...Matt. 6:9

7. Howbeit this kind goeth not out but by prayer and fasting. Matt. 17:21

8. And all things, whatsoever ye shall ask in prayer, believing, ye shall receive. Matt. 21:22

9. ...Sit here while I go and pray yonder. Matt. 26:36

10. These words spake Jesus, and lifted up his eyes to heaven, and said, Father, the hour is come, glorify thy Son, that thy Son also may glorify thee John 17:1.

11. And at midnight Paul and Silas prayed, and sang praises...Acts 16:25

12. Pray without ceasing (without continue, without stopping) 1Thess. 5:17.

About the Author

Author voice concerned about the church of God and God's people proper educational learning opportunity. As a American Baptist College seminary training and pastorial experience help to write this book.

Printed in the United States
By Bookmasters